The Perfect Heart

"...I will walk within my house
with a perfect heart."

Psalm 101:2

by

Jeri Williams

Harrison House
Tulsa, Oklahoma

The Perfect Heart
ISBN 0-89274-922-9

Cover & contents design & typesetting by: sigma graphic design • Broken arrow, Ok

Presented to

_____

∽∾

By

_____

∽∾

Date

_____

∽∾

Occasion

_____

Table Of
Contents

The Perfect Heart

Scripture Library

The numbers in parentheses following Greek and Hebrew words in this book are their entry numbers in the "Greek Dictionary of the New Testament" or the "Hebrew and Chaldee Dictionary" of *Strong's Exhaustive Concordance of the Bible,* James Strong (Nashville: Abingdon, 1890). Definitions of Greek and Hebrew words in this book are taken or compiled from their definitions in the following books: *The Complete Word Study Dictionary: New Testament,* Spiros Zodhiates (Chattanooga, Tennessee: AMG Publishers: 1992) · *Gesenius' Hebrew and Chaldee Lexicon to the Old Testament Scriptures,* (Samuel Prideaux Tregelles, trans.) H. W. F. Gesenius (Grand Rapids, Michigan: Baker Book House, 1990) · *The New Brown-Driver-Briggs-Gesenius Hebrew and English Lexicon,* Francis Brown (Peabody, Massachusetts: Hendrickson Publishers, 1979) · *The New Thayer's Greek-English Lexicon of the New Testament,* J. H. Thayer (Peabody: Hendrickson, 1981) · *An Expository Dictionary of New Testament Words,* W. E. Vine (Nashville: Royal Publishers, Inc.) · Strong.

Foreword

"In the midst of an age of turmoil, this book is a harbor of peace and a reservoir of godly wisdom for anyone who has input into the lives of growing children.

"Jeri Williams is a wonderfully sensitive woman of God whose life and teaching exalt the role of motherhood and the importance of family. This book will challenge the purity of your child-rearing motives while supplying an extremely comprehensive biblical perspective on how to meet that challenge.

"Were not one page of this book ever penned, the proof of its validity is revealed in the lives of her two beautiful daughters, Amy and Grace. Now as young adults, each one radiates the inner beauty of lives centered around a vital relationship with Jesus Christ and whose individual visions are to demonstrate excellence in all they do.

"Much fruit has also been born through Jeri's teaching in the lives of our ladies here at Church On The Move."

Pastor Daine Demaree
Church On The Move, San Diego,
CA

"I have known Jeri Williams for many years. She is a fine, godly woman who has two beautiful, intelligent daughters as a credit to her motherhood. I know you will be blessed by this book as Jeri shares her life and what she has learned from experience, and most importantly, God's Word."

Pastor Bob Yandian
Grace Fellowship, Tulsa, OK

Introduction

*O*NE OF THE FIRST COMMANDMENTS God ever uttered was that which He spoke to Abram when He appeared before him at age ninety-nine. Just as with Abram, when God calls us to holiness, He is preparing grounds for blessing.

The Lord told Abraham in Genesis 17:1,2, "I am the Almighty God; walk before me, and be thou perfect. And I will make my covenant between me and thee, and will multiply thee exceedingly."

God was asking Abram for a commitment to holy living so that He could establish His covenant with him. It was God's desire from the foundation of the earth to establish men as "earth blessers" and fulfill His promises in their lives. But He has to have willing and obedient hearts to secure His covenant. Today, He is still seeking those same contrite hearts to "walk within their homes with a perfect heart."

"For the eyes of the Lord run to and fro throughout the whole earth, to show himself strong in the behalf of them whose heart is perfect toward him...." 2 Chronicles 16:9

Why did the Lord choose Abram to establish His covenant? Because covenants are perpetual and must be safeguarded from generation to generation. There must be a passing of godly heritage from age to age before God can fully establish His will in the earth. God is still seeking upright homes that will pass "the baton" and faithfully run the race to build His Kingdom. God made His covenant with Abraham because He knew he could be entrusted to secure his descendants with a vibrant faith that would uphold his lineage until the coming of the Lord Jesus Christ.

"For I know him, that he will command his children and his household after him, and they shall keep the way of the Lord." **Genesis 18:19**

When the Lord spoke to Abraham to be "perfect" in Genesis 17:1, the Hebrew word He used was *tâmîym* (taw-meem´ 8549) which in general means *entire, full, complete, or upright*. More specifically, when it refers to uprightness before God, it speaks of being *altogether given to God.* *

I believe this "perfectness" that God is requiring of us, is none other than being caught up in "His presence," being consumed with His nature and fully immersed in His goodness. I believe this "perfectness" has less to do with performance and more to do with our driving passion for a closeness with our Holy God. This "perfectness," or "being altogether given to God," can only come from a "holy walking before Him" as we quest after His fullness with all the strength that is within us.

When Abraham ascended Mount Moriah to sacrifice his long awaited child, how was he able to say, "I and the lad will go yonder and worship?" Because being in the "presence of God" was paramount in his life, and worship surged with each beat of his heart. Intimacy with his God coursed through his being, and all else fell

* *Gesenius' Hebrew Lexicon.*

prostrate before His living God. He was perfectly assured of the goodness of his God, and knew, if necessary, God would even raise his son from the dead. He was able to perfectly trust his God, because he perfectly knew Him. He was able to relinquish every looming threat and abandon his fears for intimacy with his God.

It was in this attitude of being "altogether given to God" that Abraham possessed the gates of his enemies and began to bless all the nations of the earth. Today that same promise applies to us as we "go yonder and worship."

The Hebrew word in Genesis 17:1 translated "before" is *pânîym* (paw-neem´ 6440) which literally means *the face.* I remember as a young mother when my toddler wanted my undivided attention, and I seemed somewhat distracted to her, she would clasp my cheeks with her two pudgy hands, stationing my face nose to nose with hers. She would hold me in that breathy position until our hearts touched and the communication was made. Imagine that our God is reaching down with His holy hands, refocusing our affections upon Him and wooing our hearts to live before Him, "face to face."

There are differing connotations of the preposition "before" used in Genesis 17:1, but this one translation expresses the depth of inseparableness that He desires–"being in a position to feel the blowing of breath through the nostrils."

He is speaking of an intimacy that goes beyond prayer and even times of praise. He is calling for a posturing before His countenance where we experience the blast of His nostrils and are empowered by His Spirit; where the things of the world grow dim as we gaze upon His splendor and every enemy falls dead at our feet. He is longing to enrap-

ture us by "His presence" and draw us closer than our very breath, as we come "face to face" with His Holiness. He is wooing us to a haven of bliss where we abandon all cares and are swallowed up in the beauty of His Holiness.

It is my intent in writing this book to offer you comfort from the hardness of life that can so easily callous over our hearts if we distance ourselves from the "presence of God." It is my desire to show you scriptural steps in matrimony and motherhood that will enliven your walk with the Most High God—and that your Valley of Weeping will become a place of springs where pools of blessings store refreshing.

I pray that you will be that swallow who finds her home in the courts of the Lord, and builds her nest in the temple of the Lord, even laying her young on the altars of His Court.

"How lovely are Your tabernacles, O Lord of hosts! My soul yearns, yes, even pines and is homesick for the courts of the Lord; my heart and flesh cry out and sing for joy to the living God. Yes, the sparrow has found a house, and the swallow a nest for herself, where she may lay her young—even Your altars, O Lord of hosts, my King and my God." *Psalm 84:1-3 (Amp)*

I am most familiar with the onslaughts of pressures and challenges that confront a young woman of God who wholeheartedly aspires to please her Lord in every way. It is my desire to facilitate that daily walk which we strive to perfect before Him.

In His mercy, God admonishes older women to wisely train the younger women on how to love their husbands and children (Titus 2:4). As a seasoned wife and mother, I, in obedience to the Scriptures, submit myself to the Holy Spirit to be "His pen of a ready writer."

Say with me, *"I will walk within my house totally given to God, as only He can make a perfect heart."*

May the words that follow cushion every heartache and illumine His path of irrepressible joy, as you abide in His Holiness. May the Holy Spirit breathe upon the heart of this message and emblazon truth to fulfill your highest thoughts, dreams, and imaginations.

J.W.

Chapter 1

The Merciful Home

"As Christian families, we must address the
insensitivity that we show one to another.
The Scripture states that, 'What we do to the
least of these, we have done unto Him.'"

As CHRISTIAN FAMILIES, WE MUST ADDRESS the insensitivity that we show one to another. The Scripture states that, "What we do to the least of these, we have done unto Him." (Matthew 25:40, author's paraphrase) Have we allowed blinders of indifference and complacent familiarity to cloud our compassion one to another, dimming the awareness of our ever-present God? Has our withholding that which He has placed in our hands to give, shortened the Lord's hand to bless? Are we faithful to prepare our hearts before God, maturing in perfection, so that we can impart life to our families?

Preparing Our Hearts Before God

Several years ago, I was an altar counselor at an outdoor tent ministry. A young teenage girl came up for prayer, and I took her away from the noise of the crusade where we sat out under the stars in a nearby baseball field. I immediately became aware of her need for a "mother's love." She was so precious and innocent, full of wonder and endless questionings. As I held her in my arms that warm summer night, she began to weep and weep, as if a fountain of the deepest wound had at last found release.

As I ministered to her in the Holy Spirit, she settled into a deep peace as she unveiled her most tender heart. She shared her agonizing quest to know a "mother's love." Her mother had abandoned her at a young age, and she desperately sought this "mother's love" from her aunt who she presently lived with.

This bewildered thirteen-year old had affectionately served God from a young age, but had now become frightened by the entice-ments of worldly pleasures that increasingly lured her. She was clutching to her aunt for some snatch of endearment, but the fond-ness she sought only found indifference and bitter aloofness. She felt as if life was passing her by and was confounded by the "deadness" in her home. Why did she have to passively watch as her worldly friends had all the fun? Where was this God that she served, and how could He abandon her in such a hollow place?

She suffered long, lonely nights where she would cry out to God that her aunt would pray with her; oh, if only she could snuggle for hours nestled in her aunt's loving wisdom. She must know a "mother's love"—why wouldn't this aunt of hers confide in her and show her the way through this maze of searching? She intensely felt the onslaught of the "teen scene" feeding on her emptiness, and she desperately grasped for answers to resist its enticement.

She was determined to stand, but she had to have help. Questions, so many questions, who was this God that she served? Was this life He required only one of denial, or could He really satisfy her with abundant life, for she had never known it? Could He really take her into heavenly places? She'd never been there—who could show her the way—who would show her the way?

As the crusade came to a close, we exchanged phone numbers vowing to keep in touch, as we both knew we had heard from heaven on that baseball field.

Ironically, months before I had had the opportunity to minister to a young housewife who was totally stressed about the inadequate house she lived in. Not only was it already too small for her family, but her husband had opened their home to "an intruding relative" whose invasion meant increasing mounds of laundry and unending cooking and cleaning.

She was beginning to question the goodness of God, and the very core of her faith was being shaken as the heavens silently ignored her requests to move into a nicer home, void of the "intruder." She questioned why her God didn't answer her prayers and wondered if it even paid to serve Him.

Why did He forsake her in this deluge of frustration and unbearable hardship? Increasingly she was becoming eaten up with bitter feelings toward her husband whose "intruding niece" she considered the source of all her problems. She became calloused with anger and had lost the unction to pray in the Holy Spirit. Her fellowship with God had vaporized.

Several weeks later I was out shopping and ran into the "stressed housewife," and she happened to have "the intruding relative" with her. You guessed it, "the Intruder" was the wide-eyed niece, searching for "a mother's love," that I had ministered to at the crusade. The "stressed housewife" was the aunt that God had chosen to provide a "mother's love" for the niece. Regrettably, that "mother's love" was smothered under driving accusations against a God Who had failed to provide a new house and lighter workload.

Even though the aunt was a seasoned Christian of long standing in the church, she still had become so entrenched in her own needs that she was oblivious to the needs of those in her own home.

I often wondered how God must have felt at the aunt's unrelenting plea to be blessed, hurled against heaven's dome, right alongside her young niece's cry to know a "mother's love."

Did the aunt nullify her own prayers by an indifferent attitude of heart toward her niece? Why was she not able to have a tender heart toward that precious niece? Because she was unwilling to release that which was in her hand—wisdom, compassion, insight, comfort, etc.

Something else had gained her affection other than the treasures that God had deposited on the inside of her. She had become obsessed with the things she didn't have, and her heart had hardened over with complainings. Through unbelief, she failed to enter into the promises of God. Where was the Word of God that could sustain her in all of this heartache?

I recount this story as it is a scenario too often replayed in church families. Parents angrily thrust their fists in the face of God, deafening themselves to their children's desperate cry for help.

Marauding young people abandon their "spiritually dead" upbringings and fall prey to the more stimulating titillation of the world. Their youthful destiny for greatness is pillaged by the world's haunting claim to satisfy their dreams. This is most grievous to our Father God.

When we hurt as parents, we hurt our children, and we allow the devil to rove in and plunder their "goods." We do not have the right to splatter our children with the abuses that splash from our defeated walks with God. We will be held accountable as to how we managed our homes and impacted its spiritual fabric.

It is no longer acceptable that we withhold from each other what our loved ones need the most, when we and we alone are the ones God is looking to, to meet that need. We must not allow our hearts to harden over with complainings, encircling our families in the wilderness year after year, never entering the promises of God.

If we don't show our children a vital, vibrant God with substance that fulfills, then we can be sure the lusting god of this world will. If we withhold from our children, then they will look to the world's paraphernalia for satisfaction.

What's In Your Hand ?

"And having looked up He saw those who were throwing their gifts into the treasury, wealthy men. And He saw a certain widow who was in need throwing therein two very small copper coins. And He said, Truly, I am saying to you, this widow who is poor threw in more than all of them, for all these out of their superfluous funds threw in their gifts, but she herself, out of that which she possessed and which did not meet her need in the necessities of life, threw in all that she had with which to sustain life."   *Luke 21:1-4 (Wuest)*

Women of God, as we throw in all we have, even when we feel it's not enough to sustain our own life, the Master will look and see our giving. Our gift will become more than the treasury of wealthy men.

No matter how little we feel we might have as mothers and wives, it is more than enough to sustain life in those we love, when we offer it up to God. We must be faithful as mothers to make sure that we are satisfying the deep hungers of our children, no matter how lacking we might feel in the necessities of our own emotional or physical needs.

We must not become deafened to the "cries" of our children because we are so caught up in attending our own needs. God will multiply what we offer to Him, and it will be enough to sustain life in our families.

In the midst of pressing urgencies, we must offer up the provision that is in our hand. Even when it seems we have so little and the need is so great, yet when we are moved with compassion and choose to bless, the Lord will intervene.

We are accountable to God for our children's total well-being and satisfaction. As their "cries" come up before Him, He looks to us to bless them and accordingly rewards us.

I see so many families whose children have long ago relinquished their "cries for help," as they have too often fallen on parents' deafened hearts. Teens often resort to the solace of the world that whispers a deceiving hope to relieve their hurts.

Some mothers have lost a real sense of accountability, and rationalize on every hand the heartache and rebellion of their children, all the while holding within their hands "the two small copper coins" that would sustain their children's lives. If we will spend time listening to our children from our "heart of hearts," they will most always give evidence of their longing hungers.

So often as parents we harden our hearts, not feeling up to the responsibility of answering their needs, and consequently we close them off, "shaking the dust off our feet," and going on down the road to seek our own priorities. For after all, if there's no need, then that eliminates the obligation on our part. The problem is this road of our own agendas incessantly wanders in the wilderness and has yet to lead into the Promised Land.

We must listen for the "cry" of our children as intently as we would listen for the voice of God.

I can say without question, that children always make their needs known, and an attentive heart on our part will supply that need. The widow woman, even though she was lacking in her own substance, still had more than enough to sustain life, as she offered it to the Lord.

The Master will always see us when, even in our direst need, we throw in the "the two small copper coins" and with them sustain life in our families.

I know the privation within our homes can be so great at times that it seems we lose the strength to bless. But as we are faithful to reach out with what God has placed in our hand, then truly we will move into heavenly places and be strengthened from on high. It's easy to see in the case of the aunt, who seemingly felt she lacked all she desired, yet "in Christ," she had everything necessary to totally satisfy her niece's deepest longings. "In Christ," let us release that abundant life and usher our families into heavenly places.

Guard Your Affections

"Keep your heart with all vigilance and above all that you guard, for out of it flow the springs of life."

Proverbs 4:23 (Amp)

"Above all else, guard your affections. For they influence everything else in your life."   *Proverbs 4:23 (TLB)*

As mothers, how do we keep vigilance over our hearts?–by guarding our affections. The word "affection" is something that you are zealously attached to, an inclination or bent of mind towards an object that holds excitement. The promises of God are very appealing and once we learn of them, it is tempting to try to force God's hand at the expense of those we love. Sarah tried to force God's hand when she asked Abraham to go into Hagar, her maid. For Hagar to have a child by Abraham was not God's will, but Sarah became impatient for the promise from God to be fulfilled.

The aunt, no doubt, had a revelation that God wanted to supply her with a new home and lighten her load, but she tried to force His hand and became embittered through impatience and doubting. There was a "rest" she needed to enter into as she allowed the Word to go before her and accomplish His will.

We must guard what we allow ourselves to become zealously attached to, no matter how seemingly godly they might appear. We must never enthrone them above "His presence." We must guard our hearts with all vigilance, making sure that our zealous attachment for the "presence of God" is paramount over all other pursuits. When the indwelling presence of God holds more excitement than other desires, we can be assured that everything we do will flow out of Him.

I have been a well-intentioned mother that subtly pouted when my toddlers took shorter naps that interrupted my scheduled "personal time with the Lord." I have been a woman who exalted the pursuit of the comforts and niceties of life over the "presence of God." I have been a wife who allowed the "hiss of the serpent" to silence the quiet admonitions of my husband.

But these hardened attitudes of my heart were always clothed in the well-meaning guise of becoming more "spiritual." We must never become so zealously attached to anything, no matter how godly it presents itself, at the expense of those we love. Above all else, we must promote and exalt one another and dwell in "His presence," the source of all provision.

I remember back in my early motherhood, my family and I were secluded up in the red clay hills of Oklahoma. In the blast of winter, our electric lines would snap under the weight of the ice storms and leave us stranded for weeks with no electricity and frozen water pipes. But we could always look forward to the arrival of the hot summer season when our rural water supply would completely dry up, and again we would be without water for weeks at a time.

My husband, full of the pioneer spirit, would ingeniously rig up a pond system that allowed us to shower with green glumps of algae scum and do dishes with that "Joy shine." I was tempted to become "zealously attached" to getting out of this God-forsaken place and complained with the Israelites for being in this wilderness.

I was inclined to overlook the blessings that the Lord daily provided and in my desperate quest to move, I unknowingly dismissed myself from the "presence of God." I had enthroned H_2O above the "living water" that surged to be released from my belly. I had failed to guard my affections, and they were influencing everything else in my life.

Gradually, my gracious Father cultured a thankful heart within me, and as the years passed, those "waterless times" became times of great refreshing and the hills became alive with "His presence" as together we rejoiced in His goodness.

Harden Not Your Heart

"Therefore, as the Holy Spirit says: Today, if you will hear His voice, Do not harden your hearts, as [happened] in the rebellion [of Israel] and their provocation and embitterment [of Me] in the day of testing in the wilderness."   *Hebrews 3:7,8 (Amp)*

Read through the third and fourth chapters of Hebrews. After Moses had miraculously led the Israelites out of bondage, they were still dissatisfied with their provisions and complained against God.

Remember, whenever we complain, no matter if we think we are only grumbling against "ole Moses," we are really complaining against God and doubting His promises. If we are honest enough to strip away the facades of an ungrateful heart, we will usually find ourselves entangled in a choking bitterness that scoffs at the Lord's willingness to provide.

The Israelite's flesh was crying out for more luxurious accommodations and accusing God of withholding "good things" from them. Just like the Israelites, we can fail to enter into "His presence" through unbelief in His goodness and willingness to provide.

Notice that our hearts can become calloused over with bitter criticism and complaining, and then we are not able to hear what the Spirit is saying.

Our heart is the earpiece with which we hear the voice of the Holy Spirit. We must guard the affections of our heart with all diligence so that it does not become hardened and dull of hearing.

"There remains, then, a Sabbath-rest for the people of God; for anyone who enters God's rest also rests from his own work, just as God did from his. Let us, therefore, make every effort to enter that rest, so that no one will fall by following their example of disobedience. For the word of God is living and active. Sharper than any double-edged sword, it penetrates even to dividing soul and spirit, joints and marrow; it judges the thoughts and attitudes of the heart."   *Hebrews 4:9-12 (NIV)*

The Scripture speaks of a "rest" we can enter into. I used to puzzle over the translation of that verse that said "struggle to enter into rest." That seemed so contradictory to me, to struggle to enter into rest. But as the years passed, I realized the great struggle that existed within my flesh to submit to the Word of God and allow the Word to do battle for me.

There is a struggle with the "arm of the flesh" to subject it to the Word's power to perform in our behalf. It is as we trust in the Word of God to go before us and accomplish His will, that we enter into His "rest." We remain in "rest" as we believe what the Word of God has to say about us and die to our carnal ways to fulfill it.

As we humble ourself and allow the sword of His Word to divide between our soul and spirit, then His Spirit will judge the thoughts and attitudes of our heart, separating out that which is not Spirit and life.

Our soul can be a master at conjuring up great rationalizations to justify positions that have no valid standing in God's sight. Webster's dictionary defines "rationalize" as "to devise superficially rational, or plausible, explanations or excuses for (one's acts, beliefs, desires, etc.), usually without being aware that these are not the real motives."*

We must ever be before our Father, allowing His Spirit to divide between the thoughts and intents of our heart. How beautiful it was when I no longer hardened my heart with complainings and bitter-ness. Oh how precious when I prepared my heart to hear the Spirit's discernment of wrong attitudes and intentions.

When we allow the Spirit of the Living God to separate out that which seems to be so right with our soul and yet can be so

* *Webster's New World Dictionary,* 3rd College Ed., s.v. "rationalize."

unpleasing to our spirit, then we are filled with "His divine presence." We must cry with the Psalmist David for God to search our hearts.

"Search me, O God, and know my heart: try me, and know my thoughts: and see if there be any wicked way in me, and lead me in the way everlasting." Psalm 139:23

We must be quick to fall on our faces in repentance before God, with an all consuming desire never to cause one of His little ones to stumble out of insensitivity on our part. We must begin to praise God for our great High Priest who has gone before us to uphold us in our weaknesses.

I remember one of the clearest times I have ever heard the Lord's voice, was when He responded to a dissatisfaction I had with my husband. He said, "Jeri, if you would be the helpmate I created you to be, then your husband would not be weak in this area."

He showed me a vision of my husband's heart left vulnerable and unprotected because the rib wasn't in place. He cautioned me that I was that rib taken from my husband's side to protect and care for his heart.

He went on to exhort me that we, as the bride of Christ, can shield and comfort our groom's heart, the Lord Jesus Christ, as we prepare Him a dwelling place that is abandoned to the goodness of God. Isn't that an awesome thought? Our hearts can provide our Lord "rest" as He tabernacles with our faith.

Yes, there is a rest available in our homes that is paramount to our survival as wives and mothers. We must prepare Him a place in our heart that is compatible with His tender mercies.

Responding Heart

What a pitiful state we can find ourselves in as women of God when we do not respond to His Holy Word, when we hear, then walk away forgetting who we really are in Christ. As Christian women, we so often forget what we really look like.

Are we women who are just lacking so many things that the world enticingly offers, or are we "earth blessers," filled up with the life of God and ready to be poured out when a need arises? As the Scripture so aptly states in James,

"Do not merely listen to the word, and so deceive yourselves. Do what it says. Anyone who listens to the word but does not do what it says is like a man who looks at his face in a mirror and, after looking at himself, goes away and immediately forgets what he looks like. But the man who looks intently into the perfect law that gives freedom, and continues to do this, not forgetting what he has heard, but doing it—he will be blessed in what he does."   *James 1:22-25 (NIV)*

How had this aunt deceived herself, and how had I deceived myself? By merely listening to the Word of God and not being doers.

Philippians 4:19 states that all of our needs are met in Christ. How can we become more than hearers and become doers? We can continue to look in the mirror of God's Word so that we will not forget that we are blessed in everything we do and all of our needs have already been met in Christ Jesus' glorious riches.

"For His divine power has bestowed upon us all things that [are requisite and suited] to life and godliness, through the [full, personal] knowledge of Him."
2 Peter 1:3 (Amp)

Second Peter 1:3 states that He has given us everything that pertains to life and godliness. But we often leave out the second phrase that qualifies this provision, for it is, "through the full, personal knowledge of Him," that He supplies. It is as we continually seek to know Him more intimately and rejoice in "His presence" that we can rest in the peace of His accommodations, and it is only then that our spirits can be exhilarated to meet the needs of our families. God is calling us to take our families into heavenly places, into the Holy of Holies, into "His presence," but how can we take them to places we're not first abiding in ourselves?

Rejoicing is being a doer of the Word. Peace is a force that lets us know we have the victory. Above all else we must guard our peace and joy. God's Spirit never relentlessly drives us toward some "tomorrow land of fulfillment," but satisfies and completes our soul today as we rest in His goodness.

Kingdom Hearts

"For the kingdom of God is not meat and drink; but righteousness, and peace, and joy in the Holy Ghost."

Romans 14:17

How do we know we are abiding in the kingdom of God and dwelling in "His presence"? What testifies that we have entered the heavenly place of His Holy of Holies? One of the signposts that we are secure in our right standing with God is when we are able to refuse accusations and condemning thoughts from the adversary and dwell in peace and joy. We must become skillful at stirring ourselves up by our most holy faith, putting ourselves in remembrance of all of God's benefits.

I remember as a young Christian, I would spend time in the Lord's presence until I was consumed with His great love for me. Inevitably, I would be flooded with waves of sustaining joy and peace. I would draw an imaginary circle around myself, envisioning myself standing and reigning in the kingdom of God. As an act of my will, I would commit to not stepping outside the boundaries of His kingdom, to faithfully abide within the borders of "His presence." As the day progressed, I resisted those intrusions of the enemy that advanced against my positioning in Christ.

The priority of my day was to remain in the kingdom of God which is righteousness, peace, and joy in the Holy Ghost. Notice it's in the Holy Ghost, and no other way. All my schedules and accomplishments for the day's calendar would have to be subjected to my remaining in peace and joy. I stripped away those things that diluted

"His presence." As I became more anchored in the Lord, I added back in challenges that had threatened my posturing "in Him." In the beginning stages, I was thankful to be aware of Him just a few snatches of the day, but as I was diligent to seek His face, dwelling in "His presence" became an easy flow.

I was thirty years old before I came to know the Lord. He took me as a disheveled heap of emotions, stretched and strained at every human joint. I remember how ravenously eager I was for the Word of God and the life it brought, but a good thing turned to bondage as I rushed through the day so I could finally settle down to read my Bible.

Taxed with family demands on my time, I lived for the moment when I could escape into our loft bedroom, suspended in the still night air, and seclude myself with Bible and needle point in hand. There was something so therapeutic about meticulously placing each tiny stitch in its perfect place—something addictive about the order and control I imposed as I set each flash of colored thread into symmetry. Somehow this overrode all the vastness that overwhelmed me in the first glances of my new Lord's face. It seemed to lessen the clutter and disarray that came from losing control and letting the Lord straighten and rearrange the portrait of my life.

One evening, under protest, I was retrieved from my bedroom loft by my three-year-old's bedtime needs. As I irritably stood by her bedside, she could sense my annoyance and the striving in my soul. The Spirit of God came over her as she rose in authority and laid her softest hands on my scholarly head. Her prayers from heaven stroked my soul, melting every heartache. To her childish little mind, she had to woo me back into "His presence" where we could once again touch the pleasures that had vacated my hurried heart. She was not about to let me escape from His peace and joy which we usually cherished together. As freedom came, and I was loosed from bondage, my other daughter began to shout and prophesy from the great joy she felt– from then on out we had Holy Ghost revival.

I had never experienced such a move of my Father's great love, and now I knew more accurately what He was requiring of me–a moment by moment delighting in Him, a child-like wonder and awe of "His indwelling presence," irrespective of whether or not I had my needle point and Bible in hand. I glanced up at my treasured "loft," knowing that surely I was His "loft," and that in truth, He abided in me each step of the day.

I learned so many things that magical night–and I became more aware that whatever demands were in my life, God would be there as I rested in "His presence." I knew that life was continually proceeding from His goodness, but that I had to be flexible, yielding and ever listening for His leading and still small voice. What if I hadn't come down from the "loft" to answer my daughter's bedtime cries? I could have so easily tuned her out and never known of God's tender mercies through a pure heart that "saw the Lord."

After this, whenever I would start to become scattered or despondent, I would backtrack from my loss of composure and ponder how I had slipped from "His presence," and ask Him to show me the way back to His haven of rest, prepared for those who "see God." If I never read another Scripture verse, or stitched another stitch, I could still look into the face of my child and sense my husband's accepting touch, knowing My Lord was with me.

Today, even if my agendas and schedules haven't been perfectly met, I am still satisfied at the close of the day because I know I've reached His ultimate priority which is to fellowship in "His presence" and abide in His kingdom of righteousness, peace and joy in the Holy Ghost. I can be pleased because I know I am pleasing my God. I am dwelling in "His presence," empowered by His joy unspeakable and full of glory. I have touched His peace that passes my understanding and have blazed a path to heavenly places—and now I can take others with me.

≈≈≈

The Womb Of Mercy

There is a picture in the Old Testament that will help clarify the things we have been discussing. In the Tabernacle of Israel, God would meet with man. The high priest would go into the Holy of Holies once a year to absolve the people's sin and experience the glory of God.

In the Holy of Holies was the ark of the covenant which contained God's Words. This ark had a lid or covering that was called the "mercy seat." It was upon this lid that the blood of the atonement was sprinkled before God. At both ends of the ark were the cherubim whose wings brooded over the mercy seat and guarded its holiness. It was between the cherubim and over the mercy seat that God resided and manifested His glory. This is often referred to as the Shekinah glory cloud where the "presence of God" resided. It was from this mercy seat that God communed with man and gave His oracles to the high priest that sought Him.

One of the Hebrew words for "mercy" used in the Old Testament is *racham* (rakh´-am 7356) which means *womb* and implies a woman's tender mercies as she cherishes her unborn child.

We can see how far the devil has perverted the role of contemporary women in the abortion issue as they slaughter their own fetuses mercilessly. In a lesser degree, mothers withdraw from their children's spiritual needs and unknowingly discard them to the cold vices of the world, leaving them naked and defenseless without the Word of God in their heart.

We, as Christian mothers, must make sure that we don't send forth our children into the malaise of the sickened world without their being fully attired in the things of God. We must be faithful to clothe them with the power of the Holy Spirit.

The Lord began to minister to me about His ordained role for godly women in the home. He gave me a picture of our homes as a type of the ark of the covenant where we preserve God's law in our families' hearts. Our homes are a type of His ark, as we provide refuge in His Word and safety from the world's onslaughts. God wants to overlay our homes and cover our domestic arks with His "mercy seat" where He can make known "His presence" and reveal His glory. This "mercy seat" is a type of the tender compassion that God desires to flow from a mother's great love for her family.

It is our role as women of God to give birth in the womb of our mercy and create the *zoe* (God kind of Life) that will sustain our families. All reproduction occurs in the womb, and the patterning after the Lord we desire to see in our families finds its birth in the womb of our mercy. Any life we impart to our families must be birthed in our chamber of His mercy, one to another.

We must insure that our wombs are supple and rich with the fat of God's Word; that we are ready to release His Word into our families' needs. Just as with the priest in the tabernacle, God communes and reveals Himself to man over the "mercy seat."

He makes known "His presence," and we hear from heaven when we are merciful one to another. Like the high priest, we must release our family from guilt and condemnation, empowering them in righteousness and together experience the divine "presence of God."

Chapter 2

Building The Walls

*What an awesome responsibility we have
in fashioning that which God has placed
in our hands. As Christian mothers,
we have "little temples of God"
hanging on our apron strings.*

*W*HY HAVE I GIVEN SUCH A DETAILED description of the aunt and her niece? Because it so accurately depicts the ineffectiveness that can result from a well-meaning believer who is lacking in character. What great ravage can pass from one generation to the next because of disobedience to the Word of God on one person's part. As the old adage goes, "It is better to build children than repair men."

What an awesome responsibility we have in fashioning that which God has placed in our hands. As Christian mothers, we have "little temples of God" hanging on our apron strings. There are so many demands on our time and efforts that it's easy to become weary and tempted to dilute that which is required of us as mothers when we don't spend time in God's presence. Yet once again, the Spirit is saying, abound toward excellence, restore, repair the breaches, and grow up unto perfectness.

First Corinthians 6:19 states, "Know ye not that your body is the temple of the Holy Ghost?" The Old Testament graphically describes that literal temple where God's presence actually resided in the Holy of Holies before Jesus indwelt believer's hearts.

In order to stand, that stone temple, where the "presence of God" dwelt, had to be fortified and surrounded by the city's walls of defense. How much more should we cover and protect the indwelling presence of the living God within us?

When God wanted to restore the broken-down temple in Israel after the Babylonian exile, He first called Nehemiah to rebuild the walls of the city. *Without the walls of the city, the temple was open prey for the enemies of God.* I believe that the walls of *the city represent godly character traits* in our lives such as mercy, diligence, servanthood, etc. As mothers we must not only continue to build our own walls of character, but also that of our "little temples of God." We must be alongside them and together pile stone upon stone, so that their walls of character can stand strong and fortify that holy place on the inside of them where God resides.

Nehemiah was able to oversee the building of Jerusalem's walls because he was willing to give up his position of wealth and power in the reigning court of Babylon and humble himself to the task God had entrusted to his hands. There will be sacrifices as we devotedly set to work on our "little temples," but great is the reward.

"He that hath no rule over his own spirit is like a city that is broken down, and without walls."Proverbs 25:28

Why do we discipline children? So that we can instruct them in the Word of God. The Bible says that you can't teach a rebellious child anything. We discipline them so that they can lead orderly, fruitful lives where their spirit man rules and reigns. Let's not raise dysfunctional children who are unable to express the mercy and character of God.

In the last chapter we discussed the "mercy seat" and how we as mothers should be the covering in our homes that are ready to offer pardon, mercy, reconciliation, cleansing, and forgiveness in the power vested in the blood of Jesus.

This "mercy seat" is situated in the Holy of Holies, and we should consider ourselves as a room in God where our family can come and experience His manifested glory. God enthrones Himself above the "mercy seat" and communes with us and speaks to our hearts when we are merciful one to another.

The Hebrew word for "mercy" in the Old Testament carrying the meaning "mercy seat," #3727 in Strong, is derived from #3722. Another word derived from #3722 carrying the meaning of "mercy" is #3723, *kâphâr* (kaw-fawr´) which means *protected by walls,* as concerning a village. In this connotation of "mercy," there is an implied concept of a well-thought out preparation for future attacks. This "mercy" speaks of a planned strategy to thwart invasions of the enemy.

I feel the Holy Spirit is prompting us as women of God to faithfully build character walls in our children so that the Shekinah glory that is deposited on the inside of them will emanate to every dark corner of the earth. Like Nehemiah, we will confront many challenges and be taunted and heckled to come down from building the wall, but we must keep the trowel in one hand and a sword in the other and continue to build.

What is the consequence when we fail to appropriate the mercy of God in raising our children? What happens when we neglect building walls of character in our children to fortify them against onslaughts?

We all know the story of Eli the high priest and how "he did not restrain his sons" (1 Samuel 3:13). His sons, Hophni and Phinehas, were slain in a single day as they presumptuously took the ark of the covenant into battle against the Philistines.

The ark of the covenant represented God's manifested presence at that time, but Hophni and Phinehas' character could not validate the provisions of God. The two sons stood powerless without holy virtues, and the ark was unable to destroy the enemy in their behalf.

Eli's house was stripped of its heritage and priestly lineage. There is a "spiritual death" that occurs in our homes when we fail to fortify our children with the attributes of God, and His glory dissipates.

Kâphâr mercy is more encompassing than just being tender hearted and meeting obvious needs. It looks down the halls of time and abounds toward meeting needs with a preventative love. This *kâphâr* mercy requires a heart that is willing to seek and search for God's wisdom. Wisdom that will enable us to usher our children into "His presence." There is a power that comes from holiness, and only in that enduement from on high are young people equipped to manifest His glory.

The Stone Wall

"But the fruit of the [Holy] Spirit [the work which His presence within accomplishes]—is love, joy (gladness), peace, patience (an even temper, forbearance), kindness, goodness (benevolence), faithfulness, gentleness (meekness, humility), self-control (self-restraint, continence). Against such things there is no law [that can bring a charge]. Galatians 5:22,23 (Amp)

If we could see holiness, this is a facet of what it would look like: love, joy, peace, patience, kindness, goodness, faithfulness, gentleness, and self-control. *These are the stones with which kâphâr mercy builds the walls—walls that protect and defend the "presence of God" within our children. Holiness is rooted in the "presence of God" and laden with spiritual fruit.* These attributes are the nature of the Holy Spirit, and as godly mothers we are entrusted to duplicate these virtues in our children by teaching them to abide in "His Presence."

Notice that these fruits are a work of the Holy Spirit in them and cannot be acquired other than living in the "presence of God." It is not enough to merely legislate "do's" and "don'ts" to our children, but we must bring them into a vibrant, vital union with the passionate God. They must above all else, have pure attitudes of heart and an insatiable hunger for "His presence."

It is of paramount importance as mothers that we teach our children the attributes of the Holy Spirit. Here are just a few examples of precepts that we can implement in our daily comings and goings. *Let's take each precious stone and build the walls so that His glory may unveil in the earth.*

Stone By Stone

Love

- Teach them that love is their new nature and has been shed abroad in their hearts by the Holy Ghost. (Romans 5:5)
- Teach them that loving God is keeping His commandments and following His precepts. (John 14:15)

- Teach them that love involves rebuke and earnest correction, therefore to be enthusiastic about godly instruction and earnestly repent. (Revelation 3:19)

Joy

- Teach them that the Word of God planted in their heart actually becomes a force of joy in their life. That when they believe the Word of God, the Word of God becomes joy and the two cannot be separated. (Psalm 16:11)

- Teach them that Satan can't steal their joy unless he steals the Word out of their hearts. (Matthew 13:20)

- Teach them that joy is the barometer that reads the level of their trusting and abiding in God's promises. (Psalm 43:4)

Peace

- Teach them that peace is a place in Christ where they surrender to His will and trust in His goodness, mercy, and power. (Philippians 4:7)

- Teach them that peace is a spiritual force that confirms and testifies that they have the victory. (Romans 14:17-19)

- Teach them that peace is the umpire that settles the decisions in their lives; to always go with the "call" of the umpire of peace. It is the witness that verifies the right choice. (Colossians 3:15)

Patience

- Teach them that patience is a precious virtue that tries, proves and perfects their faith. (James 1:3)

- Teach them that patience is one of the attributes that allows them to inherit the promises of God. (Hebrews 6:12)

- Teach them to be calmly diligent, neither hasty nor impetuous, nor easily provoked. (1 Corinthians 13:5)

Kindness

- Teach them that kindness is zealous abounding toward others to show favors and benefits. (Colossians 3:12)

- Teach them to esteem others more highly than themselves. (Philippians 2:3)

- Teach them that kindness arduously moves in compassion to the afflicted and unfortunate. (Job 6:14)

Goodness

- Teach them that being good brings delight and rejoicing to their heart. (2 Chronicles 6:41)

- Teach them that they can be satisfied and filled up with the goodness of the Lord. (Psalm 107:9)

Gentleness

- Teach them that fashioning themselves after the Lord's gentleness will make them great in the earth. (Psalm 18:35)

- Teach them that the Greek word for "gentleness" can mean *to furnish what is needed* or *useful toward others* or *willing to help.* Show them how to be there for other people and supply what they need.

Self-Control

- Teach them that exercising self-control makes them mightier than a man who takes a city. (Proverbs 16:32)

- Teach them to put a watch on their mouth and bring every thought into captivity in obedience to Christ. (James 3:8; 2 Corinthians 10:5)

- Teach them to buffet their bodies and put their flesh under that they might not disqualify their testimony. (1 Corinthians 9:27)

Teaching

When I have repeatedly used the word "teach" in the above examples, it does not mean to simply give instructions to be either accepted or rejected. This teaching demands results and conformity in behavioral patterns. This teaching requires a "passing of the test" where there is a demonstration of godly attributes in the home, one to another.

"And ye shall teach (3925) them your children, speaking of them when thou sittest in thine house, and when thou walkest by the way, when thou liest down, and when thou risest up."   *Deuteronomy 11:19*

One Hebrew word for "teach" is *lâmad* (law-mad´ 3925) which means *to goad.* A goad was a rod or instrument with a sharp point used to prick a beast to move quickly along proper paths. It has the implication of teaching by using the rod of correction as an incentive. Obviously we are not to drive our children as beasts, but we are to incite, stimulate and urge them to move forward in the things of God.

"And thou shalt teach (8150) *them* (the Word of God) *diligently unto thy children, and shalt talk of them when thou sittest in thine house, and when thou walkest by the way, and when thou liest down, and when thou risest up."*   *Deuteronomy 6:7*

Another Hebrew word for "teach" is the primitive root *shânan* (shaw-nan´ 8150) which can imply to "inculcate or whet." Webster's dictionary defines "whet" as to make keen or stimulate the appetite. He defines "inculcate" as to impress by frequent admonitions, to teach and enforce by frequent repetitions; to urge on the mind. Actually the Spirit of God is calling us to whet our children's appetite for the things of God and to urge on their mind by frequent admonitions in the Scriptures.

Are we willing as mothers to pay the price for building godly character in our children? Many times it's easier to ignore their bickering than confront the root of strife. It can be very consoling to rationalize their strivings as a stage all siblings pass through, but do we have the caring foresight to sacrificially fortify their character?

I can remember some of the first times our family made a concerted effort to "seek the face of God," or as our young daughters innocently called it, have "deep worship." As we attempted to show

them by example how to enter into a time of praise, the enemy would invariably incite their fleshly desires to control all the instruments of praise–the tambourine as well as the kazoo and whatever else they could grab–while their sister stood empty-handed. It seemed as if every ugly head reared up during worship times, and it would have been easy to back off.

But resistance only confirmed we were on to something divinely inspired and most valuable. We knew if we were faithful to prepare our hearts before Him, surely we would enter His courts where one day is better than a thousand anywhere else.

Over and over, we would sit down with our children and expound on the heartache that would ensue from their not "ruling over their own spirit." We would instruct them of the heart they needed to prepare in order to come before "His presence." We would explain that they would never love anyone more than their sister, and yet they were openly devaluing her worth.

The Lord so gently exposed that when my husband and I allowed them to debase one another, by arguing and bickering, we were actually inculcating in a harmful way. We are repeatedly teaching them to become familiar and dangerously comfortable with ungodly patterns that statistics tell us are washing over into self-indulgent marriages that beach on the American divorce shore.

Don't kid yourself, if you don't teach them to cherish their brothers and sisters, they will have difficulty cherishing their marriage partners when pressures come. Unfortunately as parents, we have too often become proficient at desensitizing our children's genuine desire to "esteem each other higher than themselves."

Let us move in *kâphâr* mercy placing each costly stone as a mighty bulwark against future onslaughts. Let us cultivate that precious fruit that effortlessly yields when we abide in "His presence."

At a point in my life when I felt like a harried, worn out "taxi mom," the Lord so clearly asked me what the Bible had to say about education, sports, peer enrichment, etc. Not much! Then He said, *"Notice My focus in the Word is always to get wisdom"–"wisdom is the principal thing"–"get understanding"–"listen to knowledge,"* etc. Hundreds of times in Proverbs young people are instructed on the virtues of wisdom. Proverbs 8:11 teaches that, "Wisdom is better than rubies; and all things that may be desired are not to be compared to it."

Yet as parents, we often forsake wisdom and let it lay dormant in the wake of rising deluges of humanistic education. As we instruct our children on how to seek first the kingdom of God, then all other things will be added to them, such as scholastic achievement, intramural merits, etc. Wisdom, the Word of God, is the fountain, the well-spring from which all their accomplishments and pleasures flow.

When I was still a young mother, the Lord showed me a vision of my standing before the judgment seat of Christ at the end of my life. He was holding me accountable for my children's spiritual wisdom. I was pleading and making my case on why I hadn't invested certain godly principles into my daughter's lives.

I heard myself saying in response to the Lord's probing, "But I intended to teach them that, Lord–I just ran out of time–they grew up so fast, Lord–I just ran out of time." I remember how earnestly disappointed both the Lord and I felt, but at the same time there was a renewed surge of strength, as I knew I would have another chance.

This gracious God of mine would give me another chance. He would create and energize within me the will to do His good pleasure. Then He flashed a picture of myself as a plump mother hen brooding over my chicks with my feathers fluffed at attention. He put me in remembrance of His Holy Word.

"O Jerusalem...how often would I have gathered thy children together, as a hen doth gather her brood under her wings, and ye would not! Behold, your house is left unto you desolate." Luke 13:34,35

Surely our girls weren't as stiff-necked as Israel, and as I was faithful to gather them to the Lord, they would come. Sometimes being a "mother hen" can seem so passive and our posture so spectator-ish, but brooding over our children is one of the most miraculous events that we could ever experience. He is so gracious to let us be His co-laborers together with Him in incubating life. *Praise God! He has made a way, so that our homes do not have to be left desolate.*

"The earth was without form and an empty waste, and darkness was upon the face of the very great deep. The Spirit of God was moving (moved KJV 7363), (hovering, brooding) over the face of the waters."

Genesis 1:2 (Amp)

This phrase, "mother hen gathering her brood under her wing," has the same connotation as in Genesis 1:2 when the Scripture states that, "the Spirit of God was moving (hovering, brooding) over the face of the waters."

This word "move" is the Hebrew word *râchaph* (raw-khaf´ 7363) which means to be soft, to be moved or affected with feelings of tender love. Hence to *cherish,* to *brood over young ones (as an eagle).* It was figuratively used of the Spirit of God who brooded over the shapeless mass of the earth, cherishing and vivifying it. This same connotation was used in 2 Kings 4:34, when Elisha raised the Shunammite woman's son from the dead.*

"He went up and lay on the child, put his mouth on his mouth, his eyes on his eyes, and his hands on his hands. And as he stretched himself on him and embraced him, the child's flesh became warm." 2 Kings 4:34 (Amp)

Out of these Scriptures, the Lord clearly reminded me that it was His great love and concern for us that enabled Him to create the magnificent wonders of the universe from a formless and void mass.

He did not produce life with merely a cold, doctrinal command, but rather His Holy Spirit tenderly brooded and hovered over the face of the deep, and out of His tender mercies it waxed warm and burst forth with life. It is only as we cherish and are moved

* *Gesenius' Hebrew Lexicon.*

with feelings of tender love that we can mold and make our children in the image of God and cause them to take on divine shape and form.

He opened my eyes as to the consuming intensity that it would take on my part to raise my children from the dead areas in their lives. He spoke to me about the tenacity and relentless efforts of faith that vivifying my children would require—that I could only impart the overflow of life that I myself was experiencing.

It would take nothing less than stretching myself over them and extending myself beyond the bounds of "natural motherly affection"- that I must spread myself over them, overshadowing them in the compelling ascendancy of the Holy Spirit. For it is the ministry of the Holy Spirit that prepares for the entrance of His Word.

It wasn't until the Holy Spirit brooded over the face of the deep that God's spoken Word found entrance and light came into existence. We must minister to our children in the Holy Ghost, moving over them with feelings of tender love, cherishing their immeasurable worth. It is then when intimacy with their Father will birth, bringing life in the beauty of His holiness.

Chapter 3

What Else The Bible Has To Say About Children

"Train up a child
in the way he should go:
and when he is old,
he will not depart from it."
Proverbs 22:6

*P*ROBABLY ONE OF THE MOST PRESSING problems I see in the body of Christ today is the stress and loss of composure that comes from raising children. So many families are shaken to the core and tossed unmercifully by the dictates of uncontrollable children. This ought not to be! The Bible states that:

"Lo, children are an heritage of the Lord: and the fruit of the womb is his reward. As arrows are in the hand of a mighty man; so are children of the youth. Happy is the man that hath his quiver full of them: they shall not be ashamed, but they shall speak with the enemies in the gate."   *Psalm 127:3-5*

"Blessed is the man that feareth [reveres and worships] *the Lord, that delighteth greatly in his commandments. His seed shall be mighty upon earth: the generation of the upright shall be blessed. Wealth and riches shall be in his house: and his righteousness endureth for ever. Unto the upright there ariseth light in the darkness."*

Psalm 112:1-4

"Correct thy son, and he shall give thee rest; yea, he shall give delight unto thy soul."   *Proverbs 29:17*

"Through [godly] *wisdom is an house builded; and by understanding it is established: and by knowledge shall the chambers be filled with all precious and pleasant riches."*   *Proverbs 24:3*

Saying The Same Thing God Says

What is the solution for the restoration of peace and abundant joy in homes? It is faith in the integrity of God's Word, and that it will prosper that to which it is sent. Taking God's Word and putting it on our lips is the greatest privilege we could ever have—that a holy God would entrust us with His *zoe* life, the "abundant life" (2222) of John 10:10, and allow us to create by the fruit of our lips.

Hebrews 13:15 speaks of "offering the sacrifice of praise to God continually, that is, the fruit of our lips giving thanks (3670) to His name." The Greek word for thanks is *homologeo* (hom-ol-og-eh´-o 3670) which means: to say the *same thing as,* to *agree with,* and to confess by way of *celebrating with praise.*

It is imperative that we say the same thing that God says about our children. We must confess along with the Word of God, that our children give delight to our soul—that they are mighty upon the earth—that they fill up the rooms of our home with pleasantness. When we do this, we are actually celebrating with praise, and praise is the gateway into "His presence."

"Thy wife shall be as a fruitful vine by the sides of thine house: thy children like olive plants round about thy table." Psalm 128:3

The olive berries were the main ingredient in the preparation of the anointing oil for sacred temple use. In the Old Testament, the anointing oil was a symbol of endowment with the Spirit of God. The Scripture is declaring in Psalm 128:3 that our children are as olive plants around our table. He is proclaiming as truth, that our children are powerful instruments of His Spirit to be poured out for His purposes.

I remember when one of our daughters was just a preschooler, and it came time for bedtime prayers, her tender spirit was sensitive to the emptiness in my heart as we held each other at the close of day. I had spoken nothing about the inner despondency I was struggling with, but she was alive to my defeat and heard my silent cry.

She found her mother cut off from the flow of God's life, and with all the authority she could muster, she raised her softest sweet voice in God-ordained authority and said, "I'm going to pray for you!" She began to rebuke the devil out of my life and prayed that, *"I would know Jesus."* She began to pray in the Spirit and smother me with kisses as I wept from the cleansing.

The power of God fell so strongly that wondrous night, just with a touch from a tiny child's hand, reaching out in compassion. Of course she knew that I knew Jesus, but in her simple understanding, she was demanding a vital, breathing relationship where we could touch and feel the "presence of our God"–where He would step into our hurt and deliver us "face to face." She was naive enough to believe that if you "knew Jesus," there was a power and a force of joy that triumphed over every hopelessness–that He vitally impacted every move we made.

Heaven came down that night in our moonlit bedroom. My other daughter began to bounce on the bed shouting, "I feel like I can leap over walls!" We were swallowed up in the praises of our God as He filled that chamber with all precious and pleasant riches. Oh, how beautiful it is to humble yourself under an anointed vessel of God, no matter how childish or small that vessel might seem. How beautiful it is to believe God–take Him at His Word–say what He says–and agree with Him that our children are an inheritance from Him and His reward to us. How beautiful it is to confess by way of celebrating with praise.

≈≈≈

Biblical Discipline

Oh, how grateful I am that we disciplined our children when they did not reverence the "presence of God"–that we didn't back off when we were trying to establish times of family worship–that we saw to it that their soul did bless the Lord.

Over and over again, I encounter women who refuse to say what God says about godly discipline. They do not say the same thing that God says about spanking their children. Often they've elevated their thinking above God's Word of instruction and say they've tried spanking, but it just doesn't seem to work. "Let God be true, but every man a liar." (Romans 3:4) If God commands it, it has to work.

He did not say to only discipline your child by standing your child in a corner or giving him time out.

We do not have the prerogative to select those portions of God's directions that please our emotions. We must be obedient to the Word of God, not having an attitude of, "Well, I'll try and see if it works." Consistent godly discipline is not an option but a commandment. Here's what the Bible has to say about raising children.

"Foolishness is bound in the heart of a child; but the rod of correction shall drive it far from him."

Proverbs 22:15

The scriptural definition of the rod of correction is a flexible branch from a tree or a stick. (A wooden dowel purchased from hardware stores works great and for young toddlers, a wooden spoon, or paddle.)

Notice this rod is not your hand, belt, or the closest thing you can grab. It is to be administered by a hand of love that desires to present the Lord with a child of godly character who will glorify Him throughout eternity. This correction is to be done in private so as never to embarrass or humiliate; never done in anger or harshness, as faith works by love.

"Children, obey your parents in all things: for this is well pleasing unto the Lord...And whatsoever ye do, do it heartily, as to the Lord, and not unto men."
                                    Colossians 3:20,23

"For man looketh on the outward appearance, but the Lord looketh on the heart."   *1 Samuel 16:7*

Not only should we discipline for willful disobedience of outward actions but for wrong attitudes of the inner heart as well. Outward signs of disobedience are easily recognizable, such as temper tantrums, talking back, open rebellion, etc. But be aware of the more subtle signs of passive disobedience, such as:

- Refusing to look you in the eye during instruction, a hanging of the head and shuffling of the feet
- Answering with a muttered voice as they are walking away
- Sulking or pouting
- Complaining, fussing, and whining
- Scowling eye contact or facial expressions of displeasure
- Indifferent, condescending looks
- A "hurry-up, I'm bored" attitude during discussions

Often older children can become very clever in their guise to mask rebellious attitudes. They become masters at giving the very least they can get by with and still not be disciplined. Remember, God looks on the heart and a child should be held accountable for thoughts and attitudes he harbors. Outward obedience is not enough.

Strict standards in the development of godly character should be counter balanced by tolerance of childish ways in areas that really don't count that much in the scheme of eternity.

Discover areas that you can give your child freedom and release restrictions that are possibly there just for your convenience or personal preference. For instance, allow them to have wild times of zaniness; creative times which often include times of silliness and mess. Afford them ample liberty in areas that are not detrimental to the development of godly character. Let's not get religious on our children, because man's ways never bear witness to their hearts.

I remember when my girls were small, they absolutely loved cardboard boxes. I'm talking about large cardboard boxes like refrigerators come in. They were determined to have several of these stashed around the house. One became a drive-up bank teller intact with a slot for your bank card, and I was constantly harangued into pedaling up on their tricycle to request funds from my seven-year-old who peered through the cardboard hole.

Another cardboard box became a pet store loaded with dozens of stuffed animals that were lugged through the living room in transition while the store was being taken over by an "accessories mogul" who needed all my jewelry, perfume, shoes, and anything else that could be confiscated from my closet.

Needless to say, this did not fit in with my agenda of fresh flowers on the morning breakfast table and embroidered tea towels hung in my "house beautiful." But sometimes agendas have to give way to the gleam of enchanted faces caught up in the magic of the moment.

As the years passed and our box stash increased, I can honestly say that my craze to dispose of them abated, and when we moved from our home of thirteen years and it was agreed they should be laid to rest, I actually felt a tinge of loss.

One of the hardest challenges we will ever face as mothers is to whole-heartedly believe in Bible discipline and not back off because of our children's protesting. Spanking seems to scream the loudest claim against the fondness in a mother's heart, yet the Scriptures clearly instruct us to discipline our children.

"Correct thy son, and he shall give thee rest; yea, he shall give delight unto thy soul."   **Proverbs 29:17**

"If you refuse to discipline your son, it proves you don't love him; for if you love him you will be prompt to punish him."   **Proverbs 13:24 (TLB)**

"The rod and reproof give wisdom: but a child left to himself bringeth his mother to shame." Proverbs 29:15

"Chasten thy son while there is hope, and let not thy soul spare for his crying."   **Proverbs 19:18**

As a young Christian, I had consciously rejected the option to spank my children because of some abusive experiences I had had as a child. Consequently, at times of extreme stress, I found myself blurting out to my dazed toddler, "I don't want to be around you—get away from me—you're driving me crazy," and sobbing frantically with guilt trips like, "How could you do this to me?"

Finally a friend commented that I was mentally abusing my child and shared with me some Scriptures on godly discipline. God's Word began to bear witness against my decision not to spank.

Had I let a seemingly right motive become a source of emotional wounds for the one I loved the most, my daughter? Was I letting childhood scars scab over the truth of God's Word? Was I unknowingly compromising on my daughter's well-being? Didn't God's Word say if I really loved her I would discipline her?

Yet I still couldn't follow through with a totally confident heart. It took the final impetus out of my five-year-old's mouth who perplexedly questioned me one day, "Mom, why are other families more Christian than we are?"

I was shocked as to why she would ask such a thing.

Her reply was, "Well, they discipline their children." I didn't even know she knew the word "discipline;" she certainly hadn't heard it from me. This had to be the Lord. She was crying out from her little heart for a love that dared to confront the forces of self-will that she couldn't handle.

Young mother, I know it's exceedingly difficult, but dare to put your trust in His Word, for He will confirm it with unspeakable joy and deep abiding peace. I can assure you that moving in consistent godly discipline is not an easy path, for His way is narrow and can feel very constricted at times. But I am so thankful that my husband and I tenaciously held to His precepts and did not lean to our own understanding.

No matter how difficult we may find it to steadfastly follow scriptural patterns for discipline, the Bible gives us graphic examples of the harm and personal pain we will experience if we refuse to obey His precepts.

"And I [now] announce to him (Eli) that I will judge and punish his house forever for the iniquity of which he knew, for his sons were bringing curse upon themselves [blaspheming God], and he did not restrain them."
1 Samuel 3:13 (Amp)

God chose Abraham because he was faithful with his household and rejected Eli because he did not restrain his children. It matters a great deal to God what we do in the privacy of our homes, and it affects the call on our life and that which He entrusts to our care later on in our ministries for Him.

Biblical Training Of Children

Discipline in and of itself will just provoke a child to wrath, no matter how properly it is administered. Discipline should primarily be used as an enforcement of the retribution that comes from breaking God's Word. Exemplify to them in their youth that there are bitter consequences for crossing God's commandments, at any age.

Biblical principles must be taught if the child is to understand what is expected of him and what standards he must uphold. Often parents are heavy on the discipline and negligent on the nurturing side. Discipline should only be used to confine them to behaviors they have been compassionately taught.

"And, ye fathers, provoke not your children to wrath: but bring them up in the nurture (3809) *and admonition of the Lord."* **Ephesians 6:4**

The Greek word for "nurture" is *paideia* (pahee-di´-ah 3809) which means *tutorage, i.e. education or training* with the implication of *disciplinary correction.*

Godly discipline contains within its meaning the understood concept of prior teaching and instruction–learning with the implication of disciplinary correction.

This same Greek word *paideia* and its forms is also translated *chastening* in Hebrews 12:9-11 when God speaks of His "chastening" us and it yielding the peaceable fruit of righteousness.

"But He (God) *disciplines, corrects, and guides (paideuo) us for our profit, to the end that we might partake of His holiness. In fact, all discipline, correction, and guidance (paideia) for the time being does not seem to be joyous*

but grievous; yet afterward it yields a return of the
peaceable fruit of righteousness to those who have been
exercised by it...."

Hebrews 12:9-11 (Wuest)

Confess with me that, "I am a trainer, teacher, discipliner who instructs my children to be subjected to parental authority, so that they can in turn yield to be tutored of the Lord and partake of His holiness. God promises me that it will yield the peaceable fruit of righteousness."

Do you see the pattern? We as parents are given the honor of whetting our children's appetite to taste of the rewards that come from submitting to godly authority. But notice that discipline is but one facet.

Our essential responsibility is to initiate a love for God's Word and impart wisdom in our children.

In Proverbs 22:6 where the Scripture says to "train (2596) up a child," it *has the connotation of* a Hebrew midwife who would rub *the palate of a newborn child* with oil or chewed dates to encourage sucking. *It also means to put something in the mouth, to give to be tasted.**

The Scripture in Job 12:11, "Just as my mouth can taste good food, so my mind tastes truth when I hear it" (TLB), expresses the common metaphor known within Judaic tradition that *tasting implies understanding.*

* *The New Brown-Driver-Briggs-Gesenius Hebrew and English Lexicon.*

I recall the time we were raising six young puppies, and in an attempt to relieve their over-taxed mother, we were in an all-out campaign to wean them a bit prematurely. We mixed up baby rice cereal with condensed milk and threw in a little sugar for enticement. We gooped the mixture on the end of our fingers and they would suck and suck. It took them days before they could make the transition from sucking to licking, after all they had never licked before, and at this point had no need to.

After a few days, they would lick our fingers as we cleverly positioned our fingers closer to the feeding bowl. We lured their delicate faces into the creamy mixture, now baited with pureed chicken, and soon their soft tongues lapped from the bowl. We rejoiced in their triumphant transition from sucking to licking.

You know the Lord rejoices when we present our children to Him as youth that abide in "His presence" and know what it is to hear and obey His voice cheerfully and without delay. But first they must know what it is to quickly and cheerfully obey the Word of God that we as parents instruct. He wants us to transition them from "sucking" to "licking," to transfer the obedience they have for our instruction, to the obedience for the Word of God. Hopefully our children will come to the place where they will inform us of what the Father is speaking to their hearts, and together we will sit down to feast at His banqueting table.

There is great satisfaction in our Father's heart when that transition is made from our children's hearkening to our voice, to that of hearkening to His voice. Let's spend the time and devotion it takes to make it happen and truly dedicate our children to the Lord.

"And the Lord called Samuel the third time. And he went to Eli and said, Here I am, for you did call me. Then Eli perceived that the Lord was calling the boy. So Eli said to Samuel, Go, lie down. And if He calls you, you shall say, Speak, Lord, for Your servant is listening. So Samuel went and lay down in his place. And the Lord came and stood and called as at the other times, Samuel! Samuel! Then Samuel answered, Speak, Lord, for Your servant is listening."   *1 Samuel 3:8-10 (Amp)*

Here we see the transition that is made between hearing parental voices and the Lord's voice. Had Samuel, as a young boy, not been obedient to rise from bed three times in the middle of night, at the mere call of what he thought to be Eli, it is doubtful that God could have gotten his attention.

Children must hearken to your voice before they can hearken to the voice of God. Also, we see how Eli had to instruct Samuel in the particulars of hearing from God. Coming into God's presence is a procedure that should be taught line upon line and precept upon precept. It is the most precious legacy you could ever leave your children, and the most delicate to impart. It does not come short of your abiding in "His presence" yourself and wooing them by the most intimate unveiling of your souls one with another.

It is important to notice that Eli perceived that the Lord was calling Samuel. He was aware beforehand of God's desire to move in Samuel's life and was faithful to set an atmosphere for it to happen.

There is another facet of biblical training that is expressed as we have a clearer understanding of the phrase, "the way he should go," in Proverbs 22:6.

"Train (2596) up a child in the way he should go and when he is old, he will not depart from it."   **Proverbs 22:6**

"The way he should go" has to do with his individual *gift or bent.* In fact, the *Amplified Version* of the Bible actually states it that way. "Bent" means:

- to direct to a certain point; *as to bend our steps or course to a particular place*

- *to prepare or put in order for use; to stretch or strain.* "He hath bent his bow, and made it ready." (Psalm 7:12)

- *to subdue; to cause to yield; to make submissive; as to bend a man to our will.*

"Train up" comes from the word *chânak* (khaw-nak´ 2596). This is a primitive root that means *to narrow...to initiate or discipline:—dedicate, train up.* It also means *to put something in the mouth, to give to be tasted.** To imbue someone with anything, to

* *Gesenius.*

instruct. Webster's dictionary defines imbue as:

- to fill with moisture or saturate
- to fill (the mind, etc.); permeate; pervade; inspire (with principles, feelings, emotions, etc.).

In other words, it is our responsibility before God to create in our children a thirst and a desire to fulfill their individual gifts. It is our responsibility to put the Word of God in their mouth and fill their minds, emotions and feelings with His principles. It is our responsibility to permeate them with the Holy Ghost, so that He can inspire and prepare them for use in their unique callings. We are commanded to subdue our children and cause them to yield to the will of God and be submissive to His ways and purposes. We must narrow and restrict their thinking to the Word of God and whet their appetite, bending their steps toward a particular place, which is abiding in the "presence of Almighty God."

We must be fully convinced and inspire our children that they have a supernatural origin and destiny for greatness. If we offer them anything below what they were created to do, it will bore them. Their inheritance demands that they excel and achieve greatness.

Regrettably, there is a syndrome of boredom among our youth as they sit idly entranced in the multimedia and electronic game scene. They passively watch as reprobate heroes resound their lying claims to greatness on every air wave. We as parents have too often been found guilty of leaving our youth defenseless in their quest for greatness and have abandoned them to vicariously experience heightened emotions through cartoons, MTV., etc. We often deposit them in day care centers, children's church, after school programs, etc., expecting an institution to take the load. They can only enhance what we as parents deposit on the inside of them.

It is as we teach them to hear God's voice that He will unfold the unique purposes and plans He has for their lives. It is only then, as they hear from heaven, that they will abound toward greatness and scatter every insecurity.

As mothers, we must ask God to reveal our children's individual gifts and talents. Then we must faithfully prepare them and make them ready for use in their gifts. We must spend time together with them in the "presence of the Lord" until they confidently hear His voice, and are assured of His purposes for their life. If we spend enough time with our children, we will gradually see their inclinations and bents unveiling as we listen from our heart of hearts. We can trust their desires if their heart is contrite before us and the Lord.

Their inspiration comes from God, but the sweat comes from us. I know in my own life, I set aside my own hopes and ambitions, for a season, in order to have full impact on my children's pursuit of excellence.

Often their desires and inspirations can fall by the way if your children lack the fortitude and tenacity to bring their calls to fruition. We must be faithful to undergird their character, for it is a skillful tool essential in fulfilling their gifts.

When one of our daughters was quite young, she was mesmerized by listening to music. She was caught up in the harmonies of heaven, but when it came time to practice the piano, that was another story. There is a time when the anointing lifts and the "sweat" of our works has to take over. Her gifts had to be undergirded with diligence and a heart sold out to God's purposes before fruit could abound.

Another of our daughters evidenced strong leadership inclinations. She could be seen out in the yard carrying a large stick marching the neighborhood kids as she positioned them in her "army of the Lord." She had convinced them that she was their indisputable captain and was really quite precious in her desire to lead her battalion in the things of the Lord. But when they defected, she was most grumpy! She had a tendency to grumble when things didn't go her way, and when she lost sovereign rule in the yard, she marched right into the house to expand her domain.

My husband and I reminded her of the scriptural references to be exceedingly glad as God would not anoint a grumpy leader who led in her own self-serving ways. Believe me, Satan will vie for our children's anointing to serve him. Their gifts are irrevocable, but who will they glorify with them? Glorifying the Lord with their calls requires godly character! Honoring Satan with their gifts only takes compromise and indifference.

"Serve the Lord with gladness..."   **Psalm 100:2**

"When the people complained, it displeased the Lord."
                                        Numbers 11:1

I still have the remains of a tattered, tear-stained 5x7 note card inscribed with the above Scripture in Numbers 11:1 that we required our daughter to meditate on. My husband and I were convinced that she was a "diapered attorney" with theatrical tendencies, for there was mounting persuasive evidence that a cheerful disposition was essentially beyond her makeup. She was really quite brilliant in her cross examinations and indictments against our authority when we crossed her desires.

But after much contesting and several mistrials, my husband and I finally won the hearing. Upon losing her case, she was to meditate on this Scripture. It took some time, but I can say today that she is most cheerful, and I know heaven rejoices that she is prosecuting in behalf of God's Word.

Chapter 4

Ushering
Them Into The
"Presence Of God"

*"We must teach our children
to bless the Lord by an act
of their will. Worship
is a spiritual discipline
that must be learned."*

*M*ANY YEARS AGO, WHEN I FIRST GOT a revelation about the power of prayer, I began a disciplined act of praying an hour faithfully every day.* Many mornings it was quite gruesome with agonizing efforts to endure through each tick of the clock. There were some sweet scattered occasions where I was able to pierce through heaven's dome and touch the face of God. I earnestly sought for more consistency in this area and longed for "His presence" with increasing persistence. What made the difference? Why were some times so vibrant and others so dry? My heart cried along with the Psalmist:

"How lovely is your dwelling place, O Lord Almighty! My soul yearns, even faints, for the courts of the Lord; my heart and my flesh cry out for the living God."
Psalm 84:1,2 (NIV)

It was then, as I yearned with the Psalmist, that my gracious Lord began to unveil Himself to me. He took me to Hebrews 10:19 which was the key to entering "His presence" every time without fail.

---

* This revelation was based upon teaching by Dr. Larry Lea: *"Could You Not Tarry One Hour?"* (Lake Mary, Florida: Creation House.)

"Therefore, brethren, since we have full freedom and confidence to enter into the [Holy of] Holies [by the power and virtue] in the blood of Jesus."

Hebrews 10:19 (Amp)

As we mix our faith with the blood of Jesus, we will enter into "His presence" every time.

In the Old Testament, the Holy of Holies was where God resided and revealed Himself. This Scripture is telling us that we can enter into "His presence" by the blood of Jesus. How do we mix our faith with the blood of Jesus?

- By believing in the finished work that the shed blood of Jesus wrought.

- By putting ourselves in remembrance of His benefits and thanking Him for His goodness toward us.

As we enter into the Holy of Holies by the blood of Jesus, releasing our faith in the power and virtue of His blood, we then, with thankful hearts, come face to face with the Living God.

We desire to usher our children into the "presence of God," but how can we take a child somewhere we have never been ourselves? It's impossible! We must seek the Lord with all our hearts on personalized ways that we can more permanently abide in "His presence."

Women have commented to me that their children just don't seem that interested in praise and prayer times, and they suggest it might be perhaps because of their young age or such and such. NON-SENSE! *If John the Baptist can leap in Elizabeth's womb at the mention of Jesus' birth, then our toddlers can praise God at the mention of His name.*

One afternoon, I was rocking my four-year-old daughter in the easy chair just praising and singing to God in the Spirit. It was one of our favorite things to do together right before her nap, as naps didn't come easy for her. Her younger sister was still a toddler, and as toddlers do, she was just rambling around the room doing her own thing and, I thought, oblivious to what was going on.

My older daughter began to ask me about my songs and the praises she was hearing. I explained to her that it was a heavenly language that would allow her to talk directly to God. Well, she loved to pray to God with all her heart, so that settled it—she wanted to praise Him any way she could.

On that precious afternoon, when it could have been a screaming nap time brawl, she was gloriously filled with the Holy Spirit with evidence of speaking in other tongues, as seen in Acts 2:4,32 and 8:15. As my older daughter and I were exulting in this new-found blessing, I was astonished to hear the dearest tongues wafting from her younger sister's tiny, sweet voice. Unbeknownst to us, she had just drifted in on the move of the Holy Spirit present in two worshippers' hearts.

God's thoughts are certainly higher than ours. I would never have planned to get a toddler filled with the Holy Spirit, as after all, they are just learning to speak themselves and couldn't possibly understand. She hadn't officially gone to the altar and been saved, but in her softest of hearts, she knew God's name, and loved Him beyond description. Her spirit and His Spirit touched, and once again, God confounded the wise with the simple.

I tell all of this to encourage mothers to never underestimate the power of God in your home as you walk "totally given to God." I tell this story to exhort you to radically depart from "worldly counsel" that lurks at every corner. We must not deceive ourselves, thinking that our children are too young for anything that comes from the heart of God.

The devil knows this principle, and he does not discriminate or limit his activity when it comes to age. Pathetically, I have seen young preschoolers do vile dances and mouth profanities as they parrot the foul, fleshy stench of their homes.

Let's not be misled by the age of our children when it comes to the things of the Spirit. We must teach our children the spiritual act of discipline and focus their hearts and minds on the things of God. We must help them discover the Holy of Holies! Once they have tasted of heavenly places, no earthly manna will satisfy.

We must teach our children to reverence the "presence of God." I used to discipline my children if they would fall asleep in prayer time, or be willfully distracted. This might seem harsh, but what a payoff—oh, the ecstasy that comes from knowing your children hear the voice of God.

Seek for the tangible "presence of God" as you would a pearl of great price. Teach them the difference between prayer to have needs met and a yearning to be graced by "His presence." Expect your children to hear from God in your times of worship. Share afterwards what you both felt the Lord to be saying. Be open for exhortation and comfort to be ministered through them by the Holy Spirit. Let them know that you are needful and desirous for a touch of God through their hands.

Admonish them that it is a commandment to "Bless the Lord, O my soul." So many mothers act as if it is an option for their children to worship God and somehow down the line it will just fall in place. Not so! We must teach our children to bless the Lord by an act of their will. Worship is a spiritual discipline that must be learned.

How do they learn to be worshippers in Spirit and truth? By getting to know the One they are worshiping. They can't worship someone they don't know. Discover worship with them–take them into His sanctuary–where one day in His presence is better than a thousand anywhere else.

Don't allow your children to nonchalantly loiter in the "presence of God," siphoning off the anointing. Press them toward the mark of the high calling in Christ Jesus. Don't just give them rituals and ceremony, but draw them close to the very breath of the Spirit which quickens and gives life. Start today at whatever age they are, young or old.

"I and the lad will go yonder and worship, and come again to you." *Genesis 22:5*

Of paramount importance is entering into the "presence of God" with your children. They must be taught to reverence "His presence" and disciplined if they are disrespectful of the move of

the Holy Spirit. Do not allow them to lazily mutter "mumbo-jumbo tongues," but require excellency in their articulation of the precious breath of the Holy Spirit. Make them aware that they are calling forth the perfect will of God into the earth, establishing His ways and purposes—that they are privileged beyond measure, just to utter His Holy Words. They'll thrive on it !

Some of your most anointed times in family prayer will often be when you face the greatest impossibilities and bind together in the unity of the Spirit, worshiping the Most High God in advance, that surely "you will come again." Never be ashamed or too proud to share your deepest needs, as "little children with big spirits" will rise to the challenge and victory will ensue. Don't ever underestimate the packaging of the Holy Spirit. Good things can come in small packages.

Face To Face

"And the Lord spake unto Moses face to face, as a man speaketh unto his friend."   *Exodus 33:11*

"But not so with My servant Moses; he is entrusted and faithful in all My house. With him I speak mouth to mouth [directly] clearly and not in dark speeches; and he beholds the form of the Lord."   *Numbers 12:7,8 (Amp)*

The connotation of mouth to mouth is that of saying the same thing that God says, speaking as one voice. Train your children to say what God says and speak as one voice. They are His mouth-piece on the earth. Speaking mouth to mouth with God demands that we say what He says. Teach them that intimacy comes when we agree with God.

An example of this is Miriam, the sister of Moses whom God spoke through to accomplish His will. She said what God said at a very young age. Instill in your children God's desire to use them at whatever age they are, be it young or old.

"And his sister [Miriam] stood some distance away to learn what would be done to him...Then his sister said to Pharaoh's daughter, Shall I go and call a nurse of the Hebrew women to nurse the child for you? Pharaoh's daughter said to her, Go. And the girl went and called the child's mother."   *Exodus 2:4,7,8 (Amp)*

We see here how Miriam at a young age was instrumental in God's plan for the deliverance of the Israelites from bondage. She masterfully arranged for Moses to be raised and nurtured by his Hebrew mother, and yet remain in the Egyptian palace as second-in-command of the ruling empire of all the known earth at that time.

Teach your children that God entrusted a young girl to be a vital link in the fulfilling of His purposes in the earth. Miriam's timely obedience to the prompting of the Spirit of God was crucial in God's delivering power. What if Miriam hadn't known how to hear the voice of God? No wonder she led the women out with dancing when they finally crossed the Red Sea.

I believe she was privy to a portion of God's plans and purposes all along and was overcome with exceeding great joy as she experienced their passing over on dry land. From those early years, when she watched over Moses in the bulrushes, to the days she was titled prophetess as she heralded the Lord's glorious triumph, Miriam was speaking the will and purposes of God into the earth.

Instill Scriptures of great vision and purpose into your child's heart. They will always rise to the level of their faith, no matter how challenging the circumstances. Plant seeds of greatness in their most tender hearts; they will rise to the call!

"Say not, I am only a youth; for you shall go to all to whom I shall send you, and whatever I command you, you shall speak." Jeremiah 1:7 (Amp)

"A little one shall become a thousand, and a small one a strong nation: I the Lord will hasten it in his time." Isaiah 60:22

"And afterward I will pour out My Spirit upon all flesh, and your sons and your daughters shall prophesy, your old men shall dream dreams, your young men shall see visions." Joel 2:28 (Amp)

Be There For Them
In The Things Of The Spirit

"And the third day there was a marriage in Cana of Galilee; and the mother of Jesus was there: And both Jesus was called, and his disciples, to the marriage. And when they wanted wine, the mother of Jesus saith unto him, They have no wine. Jesus saith unto her, Woman, what have I to do with thee? mine hour is not yet come. His mother saith unto the servants, Whatsoever he saith unto you, do it."   *John 2:1-5*

Again we see that parental staging and foresight is a pattern that God uses to usher young people into the supernatural. Jesus did His first miracle of turning water into wine under His mother's spiritual insight and prompting.

She made Him aware of a need; it is crucial that we awaken our children's sensitivity to the vast numbers of suffering humanity that await the move of God's hand. The Scriptures state that we were the joy that was set before Jesus that allowed Him to endure the cross. Cultivate in your children a deep love and devotion for hurting humanity, assuring them that through the Word of God they are equipped and empowered to go in His name and deliver and restore.

Any heart will respond to this call of valiancy and greatness. As they have "a joy set before them," they will triumphantly hit the mark of the high calling in Christ Jesus. Expectantly await for God to follow His Word with signs and wonders as you incite your children in the deeper things of God.

"And the mother of Jesus was there." Whatever the cost, be there for your children in the things of the Spirit.

Fully Sufficient

As our children's mentors in spiritual truths, we must go before them and blaze a trail into heavenly places, showing them the way into the "presence of God" where they can confidently hear His voice.

There is a test I can guarantee, we, as well as our families, will be required to pass. What is this test? It is a test of the strength, tenacity, purity and integrity of our faith.

What gives us the tenacity to endure "the test," the trying of our faith? It is knowing that we are self-sufficient in Christ.

"And God is able to make all grace (every favor and earthy blessing) come to you in abundance, so that you may always and under all circumstances and whatever the need be self-sufficient (841) *[possessing enough to require no aid or support and furnished in abundance for every good work and charitable donation]."*

2 Corinthians 9:8 (Amp)

The Greek word used for "self-sufficient" ("sufficiency" in KJV) is *autarkeia* (ow-tar´-ki-ah 841) from 842; *self-satisfaction, i.e. con-*

tentedness, or competence—contentment, sufficiency. The English derivative of this word is "autarchy" which describes a nation's economic independence from imports from other countries.

Autarkeia denotes a self-sufficiency and an isolated ability to prosper. God is calling us to prosper spirit, soul and body independent of conducive circumstances or favorable relationships.

Concerning our homes, this *autarkeia* describes a place in Christ where we can stand in faith, and in Christ, have the adequacy to withstand any trial independent from our surrounding challenges. No matter how close we are as families and how attentive we are to each other's needs, there will still be solitary crossroads that we must face, one on one, with God and God alone. It is in these times that we can joyfully evaluate the effectiveness of the formative training years of our children. It is in these "testings" that we will discover if the precious Word of God is engraved on their hearts. If not, we with great exuberant joy pick up that chisel and continue to carve the engrafted Word of God.

These "testings" will ascertain whether *autarkeia* has been implanted and taken root in our children's hearts. Do they walk in an *autarkeia* mindset that is contented, knowing that every enemy has been defeated? Do they abide in a vigorous, full knowledge of Him, with a vital realization of their integration with Christ? Are they complete in His wisdom, strength and abilities, and no longer susceptible to the onslaughts of the world's system?

What criteria do we use to evaluate our children's test performance? How do we know that our training is being effective? We take account of how they respond under pressure, what choices they make when they feel no one is watching, or what attitudes they harbor when their wills cross authority figures. How do we tutor them to pass "the test"? We teach them to discover worship in the isolation of their private, intimate joining with Christ. Yes, as we train and teach our children in the art of worship, it begins with structure, obedience and precepts, and comes to completion as they hunger and thirst for His face moment by moment, independent of our promptings. We must daily offer them more than insipid, careless worship, but prepare for them a substantial banqueting table that is irresistible.

We must help them develop an appetite for "His presence" that they will feast on, even in our absence. We must teach them how to drink of His waters that never run dry. We must woo their allegiance to an Almighty God, full of awe and delight. "My heart standeth in awe of thy word." (Psalm 119:161)

I remember one of the major crossroads we encountered with one of our daughters when she was close to maturity. She had earned and enjoyed close to total freedom for some time in her lifestyle, but there came "a testing" which showed some loose ends unraveling. She was hurt and disillusioned that her parents would need to curtail her well-intentioned choices. She was as a wounded fledgling whose wings hadn't held her swift flight.

Now all of her years of upbringing were brought to the test. Was she "altogether given to God," and able to honor her parents, even when our demands seemed so stringent? She was obedient on the outside, but on the inside she was snarling at our counsel. We had done all we knew to do, but she had to have a change of heart from the inside out.

In those isolated, separated times when we as parents seemed to be so distant, praise God, *autarkeia* upheld her. It's a beautiful thing when your children have *autarkeia*–when they have an independent self-sufficiency, an isolated ability to prosper. When she was tempted to challenge our judgment and authority, her training to honor the Word of God restrained and constricted her to the path God had laid for her life. She was sustained in "His presence" and the joy He alone supplied.

Even when for brief periods of time, our relationship with our children might be weakened, their self-sufficiency in Christ will sustain them and be more than enough. It's then we know that they'll "pass the test."

Weeks after, as our relationship with our daughter was mending and her wings were spreading with vigorous strength, I noticed this Scripture she had posted on her bedroom wall.

"I see the Lord constantly before (1799) *my face; for He is on my right hand, that I should not be moved. Therefore my heart rejoices and my tongue is glad...You have made known to me the ways of my life; and You shall make me full of joy with Your presence."*

Acts 2:25,26,28 (paraphrased)

It was only then that I knew the greatness of the struggle she had endured, and how it was the intimacy that she had with God that kept her trusting in His Word in her brush with defiance.

There is a payday for parents who obey God!

Recompense comes when our children deny their lower nature, choose the truth of God's Word and unequivocally stand in joyful obedience. Our daughter had wrestled with the very depths of darkness itself and had resisted the clutches of the enemy to the core of her being. All those years of nurturing now rose up and took on life as Satan's onslaught fell dead at her feet.

I marveled at the Word that had become her flesh. My blessings had come full circle; she was now wooing me into a heavenly place as together we soared in "His presence." I was so enlivened by the strength compounding in her life that I was energized to search out Acts 2:25 for myself.

The Greek word "before" is *enopion* (en-o´-pee-on 1799) which means *in the face of, before, in the presence (sight) of*. It is a compilation of 1722. It is a derivative of *optanomai* (op-tan´-om-ahee 3700) which means *to gaze (i.e. as with wide-open eyes, as at something remarkable)*. It differs from *simply voluntary observation which expresses merely mechanical, passive or casual vision*, or *a watching from a distance*. *En* (en 1722) is a primitive preposition denoting *a fixed position (in place, time or state)...i.e. a relation of rest*.

This time, my daughter was the one that took me to higher ground, she lifted me up on her wings of praise and together we mounted up to God's throne and partook of His goodness. We dwelt together in rest, gazing upon His remarkableness with wide-open eyes, and surely He was ever before us, breath to breath, as we chose not to watch Him from a distance.

Chapter 5

The Battle
We Face

*"Can we really bank
our life on the integrity
of God's Word and rest in
the provision of His written Word?"*

*O*FTENTIMES I COUNSEL young women whom God has blessed with beautiful, healthy families and every good thing, yet they are harassed by the devil's lying vanities. They have seemingly slipped through those "everlasting gospel hands" and are held captive to hopelessness. The master deceiver of the ages has shamed them in defeat as their hopes fade and the Word of God takes flight in face of the slightest obstacle. Yet other women surmount the most devastating blows. Even though their lives are overwhelmed with "impossibilities," they are able to stand victoriously.

What is the difference? I propose that it is what we do with God's Word. *Every battle we face in this life is over the Word of God. What are we going to do with the Word of God in our day-to-day challenges?* Can we really bank our life on the integrity of God's Word and rest in the provision of His written Word? I believe that twentieth century women's battle is the same confrontation that Eve faced in the Garden of Eden. What did she do with the Word of God? *First, Eve entertained the devil's suggestion, "Did God really say?"*

"Now the serpent was more crafty than any of the wild animals the Lord God had made. He said to the woman, Did God really say, 'You must not eat from any tree in the garden'?"　　　　　*Genesis 3:1 (NIV)*

As soon as she began to doubt the infallibility of God's Word, she opened the door to fashioning the Word to adapt more comfortably to her personal mindset. She removed herself from individual accountability to explicitly obey God's instructions. *Secondly, Eve made choices according to what "looked right" and tossed God's admonitions to the wind of her own agendas.*

"When the woman saw that the fruit of the tree was good for food and pleasing to the eye, and also desirable for gaining wisdom, she took some and ate it."

Genesis 3:6 (NIV)

Thirdly, Eve attempted in her own strength to obtain what God had already freely given her. She assumed, according to the suggestions of the serpent, that God was withholding good things from her. She ate the fruit because she believed a lie that it was "desirable for gaining wisdom"; in fact, she was already made in the exact image and likeness of God, possessing His mind, thoughts and desires. No effort on her part could have taken her any higher, other than trust and obedience in His gracious provision. *Where was her grateful heart that she could eat of all the other trees in this garden of virtual paradise?*

So often women say to me, "Oh, surely God wouldn't require me to hit my child." Their rhetorical question sounds elevated and humane, but where is the instruction of the Lord in this seemingly reasonable assumption? Have we exalted our discretion beyond God's? He states unequivocally that if you spare the rod, you will spoil the child.

Yet we as women rationalize that surely He isn't expecting us, in this day and age, to consistently discipline our children. We don't respect the integrity of His Word enough to spend time getting a revelation of godly discipline and trust that the Ancient of Days has wisdom on how to raise children that desire to worship Him in Spirit and truth.

Frequently we as women lament about our husband's apparent failure to love us. But godly counsel falls on deaf ears when it demands accountability on our part. The Scripture states that "the love of God is shed abroad in our hearts by the Holy Ghost." If our husbands are born again, then according to the Word of God, that love is shed abroad in their heart, no matter how we might feel. By faith, we can rest confidently in God's great love that the Holy Spirit has deposited in our husband's heart, assured God will complete that good work which He has begun.

As women of God, let's begin to praise Him for the fruit that we can eat. Even if for a time that fruit is merely our toddler's spilled juice and more spilled juice. Let's rejoice in the little faces that call us Mom and the gift of our husband. *And if for a season, there seems to be a forbidden fruit that we can't partake of, let's trust in God's goodness and rejoice that we are even in His garden at all.*

We have all seen women forsake luscious fruits of beautiful children and homes in pursuit of that "one crunch from an apple of alluring glamour." Whether it be that extra spending money, ministry, time for ourselves, education or success, which are all good in themselves, let's not lust after that seasonal forbidden tree and lose the taste for the abundant fruits in our own basket.

Chapter 6

The Word Made Flesh

*"Jesus came as a
forerunner to show us
how to manifest His Word
into the physical realm."*

*J*ESUS CAME AS A FORERUNNER TO SHOW US how to manifest His Word into the physical realm. He came to show us how to unfold His Word in the earth and give it substance and tangibility. The same principles that transformed the Spirit of His Word into a flesh and blood baby in Mary's womb will cause His Holy Word to take on substance and materialize in our life.

He wants us to be impregnated with His "healing Scriptures" and give birth to divine health in our life. He wants us to conceive of "thanksgiving Scriptures" and give birth to His "rejoicings evermore."

He came that we might be quickened in our inner man by His Holy Spirit and be revealed in the earth as His sons and daughters. We are to exactly duplicate His goodness and meet every need. Jesus is our example, and we must follow Him, if we are to see His Word manifesting and taking on flesh in our lives.

The Conception
"In the beginning was the Word, and the Word was with God, and the Word was God. And the Word was made flesh, and dwelt among us."   *John 1:1,14*

Let's take a look at Mary as she miraculously conceived Jesus in her womb by faith. All she had was a rhema Word from an angelic messenger that the Holy Ghost would overshadow her, and she would bear the Son of God.

How did Mary conceive? How did she yield her womb to incubate the Word of God? How did the Word of God that is Spirit, take on flesh and dwell among men? It was all done by faith!

Even the God of the universe needed a co-laborer to manifest His will in the earth. He is still seeking those who will give birth to His Word in the earth by faith. The virgin Mary had hold of a principle that allowed the living Son of God to be birthed against all human feasibilities. In spite of overwhelming odds of impossibilities, and no other capabilities than a pure and believing heart, Mary stood at attention to obey the spoken Word of God.

"And Mary said, Behold the handmaid of the Lord; be it unto me according to thy word. And the angel departed from her."   **Luke 1:38**

We must cry along with Mary, "Be it unto us according to Your Word." We must become pregnant with the promises of God. We must be bond-servants along with Mary and believe what the Word of God has spoken to us. We must allow God to impregnate us by the Spirit of His Word and faithfully carry it full term until we give birth to the fullness of Christ in the earth.

"But without faith it is impossible to please him; for he that cometh to God must believe that he is, and that he is a rewarder of them that diligently seek him."   **Hebrews 11:6**

What is this God kind of faith? I propose it is acting on the Word of God, being a doer of the Word of God. So we could say it this way, without acting on the Word, it is impossible to please God.

Mary pleased God when she said, "Be it unto me according to Your Word." Mary acted on the Word of God when she spoke, "Be it unto me according to Your Word." Mary breathed upon the spoken Word of God with faith from her own lips and conception took place.

She became pregnant when she believed the spoken Word from heaven and it became the living Word, taking on the flesh of Jesus Christ. Life is produced when we act on the Word of God. There is power inherent in the written Word of God to create the miracles we all need. It will produce in our hearts the thing He promises. His Words are the living *zoe* life of God that inherently contain all the power of the Godhead, just awaiting our breath of faith. Like Mary, let us allow His Word to take on substance and manifest itself in healing, deliverance, peace, and anointing.

Practically speaking, how do we become doers of the Word and put action to the Word? I suggest to you, that often it is nothing more than rejoicing in our position in Christ.

"In every thing give thanks: for this is the will of God in Christ Jesus concerning you."   *1 Thessalonians 5:18*

Being a doer of the Word is not always a physical act, but often an attitude of the heart. As we make our thoughts become agreeable with God's Word, then we elicit the "rejoicings evermore" that He requires of us.

Let's think about it: if a wealthy heir promised you millions, would you rejoice now or wait until you had it? Of course, you would begin to rejoice the minute you believed it was true. The Bible instructs us of many blessings that have already been released in Christ; and as we rejoice in their truth, our faith is activated and we become doers of His Word.

It's highly improbable that we are believing God's Word when we don't have joy. Faith and depression are counter forces that cannot co-exist at the same time.

Our joy is a signpost that we are being a doer of God's Word. Once the Word of God takes root in our hearts, it becomes joy. Joy is a force of strength and invincibility that measures our faith in the Word of God. Faith in the Word of God and joy are inseparable. Once the Word of God takes root in our hearts, it produces joy.

That's why the devil can't steal the Word without confiscating our joy. He's after the Word of God on the inside of us; if he can steal our joy, then he can loot the Word right along with it. Joy and believing the Word of God are inseparable!

Continuing To Full Term

"And Mary said, My soul doth magnify the Lord, and my spirit hath rejoiced in God my Saviour." Luke 1:46,47

We see in the above verses that Mary did not wait for physical signs in her body to confirm that she really had immaculately conceived before she began to rejoice.

The immaculate conception never would have come full term had Mary not trusted completely in her Father's Holy Word and chosen to quiet the outcries of impossibilities. We see that she immediately began to magnify the Lord with her soul and rejoice in her spirit man.

Notice that rejoicing is a spiritual act that only comes from an unquestioning belief that God's Word is true in our behalf. God has called us to give birth to His promises in our private womb of faith. His blessings for our lives cannot be conceived in any womb other than our own.

I often wonder what would have happened if Mary had commented, "I really would like to bear Your Son, but Joseph will never go for this. And what about my marriage, God?–You're ruining my wedding plans." We see that Mary had to have a relentless trust in God's goodness toward her and an unquenchable desire to move in His ways and not her own.

The Birth

Although Mary had unwavering faith to believe God's Word, there were still obstacles that attempted to hinder the delivery of baby Jesus to Joseph and Mary.

"Because Joseph her husband was a righteous man and did not want to expose her to public disgrace, he

had in mind to divorce her quietly. But after he had
considered this, an angel of the Lord appeared to
him in a dream and said, Joseph son of David, do not
be afraid to take Mary home as your wife, because
what is conceived in her is from the Holy Spirit."
Matthew 1:19,20 (NIV)

When Mary had done all she knew to do, then God intervened
with His angelic host to perform His Word. God will move heaven and
earth to show Himself strong in behalf of those who are obedient to
His Word.

"When a man's ways please the Lord, he maketh even
his enemies to be at peace with him."   Proverbs 16:7

I remembered how liberated and empowered I felt when I
started walking in this Scripture. The enemy will lie to us and make
us feel utterly captivated and shackled by the spiritual apathy of our
homes, churches or nation. He is an expert in making us feel helpless
in the wake of the spiritual slothfulness in our surroundings. He is a
master at inducing fear about how others' spiritual insensitivity will
hinder God's will for our lives.

It's tempting to blame others for the promises of God not being
produced in our lives, but in truth, we must focus on our own individual personal obedience to His Holy Word. Mary could have so

easily judged Joseph for his lack of assessment of the situation, but she stayed riveted to God's promises–His Word was without reproach.

Hadn't He sworn by Himself that He would make our enemies at peace with us–when our ways please Him? And Mary's ways pleased Him! His Word was forever settled–He would cause her enemies to be at peace with her, whether it was within her own family such as Joseph, or the oppressive authority of evil King Herod. God would send His angels to hearken to the voice of His Word, and the heavenly host would go before Mary to protect and fulfill His Word.

It is no different with us, women of the Lord. Let's rise up strong in the Lord and leave every encumbering excuse behind, knowing with confidence that God will intervene in our families, even if He has to send angels to uphold the execution of His will and purposes. Let us be like Mary and please Him, so that He can make our enemies to be at peace with us.

It is time that we stop wading through prolonged scenarios on countless abuses and suffered wrongs we are encountering at the hands of our spouses and children. It is easy to score our families' faults and inadequacies and pompously tally their slips. We can neatly package an indictment of our insurmountable home environment, but can we praise God for an answer? We are quick to hurl profuse accusations and railings, but can we settle down in faith and be attentive to what God's Word has spoken to our hearts?

The depth of suffering we experience at home can be so intense, but He upholds "all things by the word of his power" (Hebrews 1:3) and our homes, like Mary's, will be upheld no other way. Sympathetic agreement with hopeless predicaments will in no way alleviate the pain.

Jesus wants us riveted to His promises. His Word is without reproach, and He has sworn by Himself that He will make our enemies to be at peace with us when our ways please Him. There are no exceptions or hard cases that warrant disqualification. His Word is forever settled; there are no "buts" in the "kingdom of God." We must focus on our ability to affect the path of our life by our individual personal obedience.

All through Scripture, angels are seen as instruments of praise and worship. Innumerable companies of them encircle the throne of God to exalt and honor Him. They by nature are attracted to environments of praise. If we desire angelic intervention, we must cultivate grateful hearts that rejoice in the revealed Word of God.

"Bless (affectionately, gratefully praise) the Lord, you His angels, you mighty ones who do His commandments, hearkening to the voice of His word."

Psalm 103:20 (Amp)

"My God hath sent his angel, and hath shut the lions' mouths, that they have not hurt me."   *Daniel 6:22*

"The Angel of the Lord encamps around those who fear Him [who revere and worship Him with awe] and each of them He delivers."   *Psalm 34:7 (Amp)*

Whom do the angels encamp around? Those who worship God with awe. Whom do the angels deliver? Those who revere the Almighty. If we have some lions roaring around our homes whose mouths need to be shut, then we must proclaim with Daniel, "He has shut the lions' mouths, and they have not hurt us."

Do we want to see the written Word of God take on substance and manifest blessings in our homes? Then let's command our soul to bless the Lord at all times. Let's put ourselves in remembrance of all of His benefits and glorify the Lord for His great goodness toward us so that He can loose the angels to make our enemies be at peace with us.

Chapter 7

There Are No "Buts" In His Will

*"Let us enliven
our families with
the truth of God's Word
as a standard for reality."*

*"We also know [with settled and absolute knowledge]
that we have [granted us as our present possessions]
the requests made of Him."*   **1 John 5:15 (Amp)**

*"...he who has a glad heart has a continual feast
[regardless of circumstances]."*   **Proverbs 15:15 (Amp)**

WHERE DOES THIS GLAD HEART COME from, which is the strength of our life? This joy is a knowing that God has heard us and watches over our every concern and has already gone before us in provision for our obedience. What is the reward for obeying God and diligently seeking Him?

As women, our reward has to do with a home full of laughter, deep intimate fellowship one with another, a husband who safely trusts in our value more than rubies, children who esteem us higher than themselves and comfortingly support as our refuge from the hardening world.

Instead our homes have become arsenals of hurling accusations, boot camps for self-indulgent relationships, and mess halls for every evil work because we tolerate strife and disgruntled hearts of ingratitude. Can we really take God at His Word and walk out of a defeated existence manipulated by every whim of the master deceiver? I state unequivocally, a resounding "Yes."

There are no "buts" concerning God's will. Most Scriptures don't qualify promises to us according to what our husband, children, etc. are doing or not doing. We are individuals who will stand before God as separate entities, accountable for what we and we alone did with the Holy Word of God.

Did we seek for it with our whole heart as a treasure more valuable than fine gold, or were we too overwhelmed by the pressures of the enemy to lift our voice in praise to the Giver of Life? Were we too short-sighted to exult the One Who will not withhold any good thing from us and promises to cause our enemies to be at peace with us?

Most mothers, at some time, have felt forsaken by the illusive dream of aproned morning kisses, childish laughter amidst rose-laden picket fences, and lulling moonbeams shed across an undefiled bed. What happens when the promised bliss of matrimony becomes misery and motherhood unfolds into an unending maze of disillusionment?

In these times of temptation, we must not be forlorn. First Peter 3:6 states that we can be the true daughters of Sarah if we don't give way to hysterical fears or let anxieties unnerve us. We must run to the One Who has gone before us and took upon Himself our every heartache and sorrow. He promises that no temptation will be irresistible, for He will show us a way of escape.

"Many others have faced exactly the same problems before you. And no temptation is irresistible. You can trust God to keep the temptation from becoming so strong that you can't stand up against it, for he has promised this and will do what he says. He will show

There Are No "Buts" In His Will

you how to escape temptation's power so that you can bear up patiently against it."

1 Corinthians 10:13 (TLB)

We must begin to rejoice that our name is written in the Lamb's book of life and be exceedingly glad that God has made a way of escape through the shed blood of Christ. Jesus, our forerunner, has gone before, perfectly pleasing the Father in every way, being totally obedient; so that in Him and through Him we could be equipped to be doers of His Word, fulfilling His will for our lives.

What did Jesus do with the Word of God when faced with the greatest battle of His life? He did exactly what we too must do if we are to triumph–He testified as to what the Word had prophesied concerning Him: that God would not leave His soul in hell, neither would He let His Holy One see corruption. (Psalm 16:10)

How does this relate to us practically on a day-to-day basis? *It means that we must live and think prophetically if we are to overcome the wiles of the devil.* We must see our children and husbands as God sees them. We must prophesy over one another by speaking out what the blood has wrought in our lives.

"And they overcame him (the devil) *by the blood of the Lamb, and by the word of their testimony; and they loved not their lives unto the death."*   *Revelation 12:11*

"...for the testimony of Jesus is the spirit of prophecy."
Revelation 19:10

We overcome in our homes by testifying about the efficacy of the blood of Jesus in our loved one's behalf and respond accordingly. We must be women of vision, confirming our confidence and assurance in our family by speaking God's Holy Word as final, undisputable authority against the delusions of the enemy.

The Double-Minded Man

In the book of James there is a man the Bible says, "Should not think he will receive anything from the Lord." *The Amplified Bible* states it this way, "Let not such a person imagine that he will receive anything [he asks for] from the Lord."

This immediately got my attention. Who is this man that God says should have no hope in getting his prayer answered? I want to know, don't you? I want to make sure I am not this type of man. I want to guard against being this double-minded man.

"That man should not think he will receive anything from the Lord; he is a double-minded man, unstable in all he does." **James 1:7,8 (NIV)**

I had always thought this double-minded man was the one who asked for wisdom and doubted that God would give it to him. He is, but there's more to it. God began to open my eyes that I was this man when I did not consider it pure joy when I was facing trials and needed wisdom.

Yes, He would give me the wisdom on how to triumph in my trial, but only when I asked in faith. How could I be assured that I was in faith, so I could be confident He would give me wisdom? Only by rejoicing in the midst of the trial. Who is the man that will not receive anything from the Lord? He is the double-minded man who is wavering in his faith to receive answers.

"Only it must be in faith that he asks with no wavering (no hesitating, no doubting)."   *James 1:6 (Amp)*

How do we know we are in faith when we ask for wisdom? Joy is our signpost that we are in faith and can expect an answer. Verse 2 delineates the man who will get his answer: it is the man who considers trials joyfully.

"Consider it wholly joyful, my brethren, whenever you are enveloped in or encounter trials of any sort or fall into various temptations."   *James 1:2 (Amp)*

Why can I rejoice? Because verse 4 states that when I persevere, then patience will have her perfect work, and I will submerge mature and complete, not lacking anything. Isn't this something to rejoice about, that we will be perfect and complete, not lacking anything?

When we lose our joy, we are actually pouting before God, and we allow what feels good for the moment to take priority over our becoming mature in Christ.

"Because you know that the testing of your faith develops perseverance. Perseverance must finish its work so that you may be mature and complete, not lacking anything." *James 1:3,4 (NIV)*

God Is Tempting Me?

"When tempted, no one should say, 'God is tempting me.' For God cannot be tempted by evil, nor does he tempt anyone; but each one is tempted when, by his own evil desire, he is dragged away and enticed."
James 1:13 (NIV)

One of the main problems in godly homes is the flippancy with which we denounce God's provision for our needs. Our ungrateful hearts often irreverently rebuke our loving Father for what we mistakenly assess as His divine indifference to our needs.

We often harbor a subtle spirit of criticism and indict a God Who would test us with such unbearable hardships. But all the while, the Scriptures state, "God tempts no man with evil, but we are drawn away by our own lusts."

Why are we so quick to place the fault with anyone other than ourselves and so eager to impute guilt to God? Because testing requires resistance, and resistance requires that we submit ourselves to God. It is much easier to accuse God than submit to Him, but when we blame God or others we have no resistance to tests. The more we are submitted to God, the better we can resist trials. Trials necessitate perseverance and accusing God comes much easier than developing the virtue of endurance.

It can be more comfortable for us to use circumstances as a scapegoat, avoiding all threats of responsibility, rather than dare to scrutinize our hearts under the examination of the Holy Spirit. The power that works within us is sufficient to override every obstacle, and when we are in an attitude of rejoicing, it is impossible to blame others for our problems.

Who is this who will never get his prayers answered? He is the one who says "God is tempting me–or my children, wife, husband, etc., are the cause of my problems–or if it weren't for such and such, I would be happy."

He is the one who presumes God has slipped from His throne. Rather than grabbing hold of heaven in times of trial, his accusing hand lies lifeless in the wake of rationalizations. He is the one who thinks contrary to the Word which declares we are "enticed or drawn away by our own evil desires." He is the one who does not consider it joy when he falls into temptations.

The Perfect Heart

God always leaves us examples in the Old Testament to pattern ourselves after and in His mercy offers them as living epistles for our wisdom. In Genesis chapter 37, we see the story of Joseph and how he was able to keep himself in a place to be greatly blessed of God. His very name means, "May God add." Through a God-given dream, Joseph was able to save the national seed of Israel from extinction. God entrusted Joseph with the fulfillment of His covenant, to bless the whole earth through Abraham's seed.

Over and over, Joseph was put in situations where he could have easily succumbed to evil, but he was never "drawn away or enticed by his own lusts." Countless times he could have embittered himself against his family, as they seemed to defy the fulfillment of his God-given dream on every hand.

Joseph was always able to identify with and draw strength from His God rather than his family or circumstances. When he was cruelly sold into slavery by his brothers, he was intensely confronted with temptation: temptation to give up his God-given dream for greatness, temptation to become bitter, and temptation to accuse the brethren.

But perseverance always outlasts persecution, and Joseph never relented in his reliance on God, even in his unjust imprisonment. Greatness requires training, and after Joseph, for 13 years, resisted the rages of pride and lusting within him, God exalted him as second-in-command over all the known earth at that time.

We too can be like Joseph and release our families from guilt. Joseph could have chosen to stand before God on judgment day and say, "Gee, God, I really wanted to fulfill the vision You had for my life, but You should have seen what my brothers did to me, not to mention Potiphar's wife." But Joseph chose to serve and bless God no matter how insurmountable his circumstances were.

Joseph always rose to the level of his faith and so will you! No one in your family can hold you down, but rather you will lift and bless them. Because Joseph went in and took the "goods" for his family when they were unable to catch the vision, God prospered whatever he did.

"The Lord was with him and made whatever he did to prosper." Genesis 39:23 (Amp)

Joseph had such deep love for his brothers, even after they wronged him, that he compassionately wept over them at their reunion. He was consumed with preserving his family's lives and being a blessing.

One of his most sterling attributes was that he released his family from guilt over the evil they had done to him. He was deeply concerned that his family not be scarred from their sin. He was compassionate about them and forgot about himself as he was confident he was in God's hands.

"But now, do not be distressed and disheartened or vexed and angry with yourselves because you sold me here, for God sent me ahead of you to preserve life." Genesis 45:5 (Amp)

"And get your father and your households and come to me. And I will give you the best in the land of Egypt and you will live on the fat of the land."

Genesis 45:18 (Amp)

Let's be like Joseph and put away hurts and wounds making a way for even those who have abused us to taste of the richness of God's mercy extended through us. So often in families, God appoints "forerunners," so to speak, who are equipped to go before and provide for others in their household. God used Joseph to go into Egypt and procure "life" in a time of famine.

Only men and women of greatness release people from guilt and condemnation. Even though Joseph's family made it tough on him, he always rose to the level of his faith and so will we. Like Joseph, God will cause us to be fruitful even in the land of our affliction. Let's go before our families, be forerunners in the things of the Spirit and cause them to live on the fat of the land!

I remember one of the most poignant moments in my life was on one of my birthdays. In our young struggling family, there was no overflow for indulgence of gifts, but out of my daughter's deepest desire to bless me, she laboriously fashioned a passionate note from the rush of her spirit man. I still cherish this card today, as I sense the faithfulness of His Word to minister to a young seven-year-old through an imperfect, yet aspiring mother.

At that time in the rearing of my children, I sometimes responded in pressured moments with abrasive remarks left over from the roughness of my childhood, but my daughter looked upon my heart and only what the Lord said about me was life to her.

In her childish handwriting, she had copied this Scripture in her hand-made birthday card, *"You open your mouth with godly wisdom and in your tongue is the law of love and kindness."* *(Proverbs 31:26)*

This was not a confession of faith, but the living, breathing reality of who I really was to her. Those screaming outcries of my old man were dead to her. Her prophetic words about me, empowered me to be who I really was. Because her simple, dauntless faith saw me as a woman of God, then I was able to become who her pure heart knew I was all along.

We must enlarge our conceptions of confessions and expand into the *zoe* life of who we really are in Christ. *"As he is, so are we in this world."* (1 John 4:17)

Let us enliven our families with the truth of God's Word, not as a formula for change, but as a standard for reality. As we release God's Holy Word in their behalf, we empower them to be who they really are.

I am firmly convinced that righteousness awareness, one to another, is the hope for godly homes. So many women feel helpless in meeting the requirements for scriptural homes, but if we walk in the truth that surely we have been translated from darkness to light, then light will arise in the darkness.

Let's empower our families to become who they really are by releasing them from the guilt of shortcomings. Let's see them free from the curse of the law which is "the falling short of the glory of

God." Jesus broke the curse of the law which is "the falling short of the glory of God." In Him we always measure up!

Chapter 8

Worthiness

*"Our self-worth and
self-confidence
as Christian women
can be found in
no other source
than God's Word."*

*W*HERE DO WE FIND OUR SELF-WORTH and self-confidence as Christian women? I believe with all my heart that it must be from God's Holy Word and can be found in no other source. In this day, with so many unattainable standards set by this world's heartless expectations, we must find our worthiness in the truth of God's Word.

I have seen ordinary women feel beautiful in Christ; I have seen simple-minded women wax brilliant in Christ; I have seen discarded women feel precious and valuable in Christ. And yet, I have known excessively blessed and capable women, who are not applying the Word of God to their lives, become trapped in "black holes" of endless despair. Their hunger for acceptance relentlessly drives them in desperate strivings for the world's applause that never claps loudly enough.

The devil's strategies haven't changed over thousands of years: he is still in the business of luring women away from the Word of God and making them discontent with who they are. Once he masterly enticed Eve from obeying what God had instructed. He instigated distrust in her heart when he caused her to dispute God's authority with one little question, "Has God really said?" As quickly as Eve began to question God, her confidence was shaken and she was set on a striving course to prove her self-worth to God and man.

Without God's Word reigning supreme in our hearts, our self-image diminishes, and we stand naked in our humanity, stripped of His glorious covering. When we reject God's Word, we feel a sense of rejection ourselves. We feel rejected because we have first denied and rejected God's counsel.

No amount of human love, beauty, wealth, or accomplishments can substitute for the value and preciousness that obedience to the Word of God imparts. As soon as Eve disobeyed God, she "was ashamed" and tried to cover herself and hide from God's presence. Women today still try to cover themselves and hide from the presence of God. As contemporary women in the glitz of dazzling feministic expectations, we must rest confidently in who and what the Word of God says about us.

What we do with God's Word is what we will do with ourselves and others. If we value God's Word, then we will value ourselves and others.

However, if we reject God's Word as final authority in our lives, then we will ultimately reject ourselves and others. If we let acceptance by others, whether the world, close friends, or family, set the standards of who we are, then we can be sure our self-image will tarnish in the light of the world's scrutiny.

We could find ourselves orphaned from our loving Father and drawn away by the accuser of the brethren, Satan himself. Let's not prostitute ourselves and allow the devil to become our agent, pandering to our "old nature's" inadequacies. For Satan will gladly sell our God-given preciousness, merchandising our "royalty" for his "servitude," enslaving us to the captivity of his expectations. He desires to victimize our self-image, subjugating us to his relentless taunts of inadequacies.

Satan has always considered himself the most beautiful of creations, and in his estimation, no one else measures up to his brilliant magnificence. In Isaiah 14:13, he declares that he will exalt himself above God's throne and sit on "the mount of the congregation, in the sides of the north." This mount signifies "the place of control."

Satan's agenda is to establish himself in a position of control when it comes to our self-image. He is driven by vanity and pride to mercilessly manipulate us, restraining the very life and glory of God destined to flow from our being. We have truly been made in the exact likeness and image of Almighty God; let us never abdicate our position in Christ.

≈≈≈

God Always Comes For His Word

Let's take a look at the One Who was victorious in all instances and in every manner. Even He, Jesus Christ, was required to be meticulously obedient to the Word of God, so that the will of His Father could be accomplished. Jesus, abandoned by heaven and earth and spurned by God and man, had to trust the Word for His very life. Even the spotless Lamb of God, the incarnate Son of God, was required to use His faith and act on the Word of God. There is no other way! We must be doers of His Word to fulfill His will.

All the hordes of hell were unleashed on Jesus, in Satan's attempt to strip Him of His worthiness before His Father. Even when Jesus became the embodiment of sin and was disfigured beyond recognition, even when He was scorned and mocked by the despising crowds, and the Father was forced to turn His face in shame–even then, Jesus had worthiness because of the Word of God stored in His heart.

In His time of gravest passion, Jesus was left only with His obedience to the Word of God and faith in the character of His Father—but that was sufficient.

In total desperation He cried, "My God, my God, why hast thou forsaken me?" (Matthew 27:46) No resounding answer bolted from heaven, but Jesus answered Himself from the prophetic Word written about Himself, that when He cried unto God, God would hear Him. (Psalm 22:1,24)

When the heavens seemingly stand silent, we must be like Jesus and answer ourselves from the written Word of God.

What gave Jesus this unshakable self-worth and confidence that His God would hear Him? Even though no man deemed Him lovely or pleasing, yet He still fulfilled the will of God for His life. His confidence and self-worth were forever settled in the Scriptures and what God had written about Him. Even when His heart was melted with anguish, and His tongue cleaved to His jaw in thirst, and He was brought to the dust of death, He still knew God would come for His Word.

When every fiber of His being was crying out that His God had forsaken Him, yet He knew, along with the prophetic Psalmist, that "when He cried to God, He heard Him." He knew that although men despised and ridiculed Him, His Father would come for His Word that He had stored in His heart.

"For he hath not despised nor abhorred the affliction of the afflicted; neither hath he hid his face from him; but when he cried unto him, he heard."   **Psalm 22: 24**

A more in-depth look at the original Hebrew in Psalm 22:24 would render the following paraphrase:

"God will not raise His head loftily and disdainfully and consider me unworthy of His character or deem me unworthy of His notice or care, nor will He loathe my impure cry when I am depressed in mind or circumstances; neither will He hide His face from mine in times of worship or battle; but when I cry unto Him, He hears me."   **Psalm 22:24 (paraphrase)**

Just as we do, Jesus had an opportunity to let His senses overrun the Word of God. Yet He knew with total assurance that what the Father had spoken about Him was resounding in the eternal halls of glory, and that every jot and tittle would be fulfilled as He stood in agreement.

No matter how many times we feel inadequate or lacking— no matter how loud the world screams, "You're not enough," God will always hearken to the voice of His Word. God always comes for His Word! He always hearkens to the voice of His Word uttered on our lips of faith.

Even Jesus, when He became sin and embodied the gross vileness of all humanity and desecrated that which was holy, even then, the Father was beholden to His Word when Jesus spoke in faith and praised God for answered prayer while He was still on the cross.

Jesus arose from the prostrate circumstances of death and hell by believing what the Word of God said about Him. *His being a doer of the Word gave entry for the Holy Spirit to move in His behalf.* This is the pattern for our lives, we must put faith into what the Word of God says about us.

Women of the Lord, God has spoken some prophetic words about us. It is time we pick up these Holy Words and breathe life into them by faith in the Son of God and His finished work on Calvary, so that we too can be raised from the dead circumstances of our predicaments.

We must arise and shine for His light has come, and truly His glory has risen upon us. Have we poured out our own blood to the point of death? I don't think so. *Let's refuse to be spiritual wimps any longer and rise to the high calling of Christ.*

It's time as prodigal children we run headlong into the arms of the living Word and find comfort in His wisdom. It's time we let His recognition, and His alone, satisfy our hunger for acceptance. It's time that we feel beautiful in His sight like He says we are. *It's time we stop letting the world's conception of us dictate our fulfilling the will of God for our lives!*

If Jesus was resurrected by having faith that what the Word of God said about Him was true, then is there another way for us? Absolutely not! We must be doers of the Word, remembering that all of God's power is in His Word. We must give the Holy Spirit something to execute in the earth, and allow Him to raise us up from any death in our lives.

How many of us have been poured out like water; had all of our bones out of joint, and our heart melted like wax from anguish? (Psalm 22:14,15) It may seem at times that we have, but often it takes no more that our husband's curt remark, ten extra pounds, or a "glance in the mirror" to send us to the depths of insecurity.

We must remember that Jesus has suffered far beyond what any of us will ever experience. He was marred beyond recognition that we might be spotless and perfect. *He went before us to test and prove the validity of His Father's Word, to substantiate beyond dispute that the Word of God can uphold, even to the point of death.*

Jesus quoted from Psalm 22:6 that, *"He is a worm, and no man; scorned of men and despised by the people, yet His Father does not consider Him worthless."* What enabled Jesus to have this incredible self-worth and total confidence when all the world shouted Him down in scorn? It is the same confidence that we can have as covenant children.

Because we consider the precious Word of God as true in our behalf, we can know with assurance that God is moving in our behalf. Even in the midst of apparent abandonment and worthlessness, we must pattern ourselves after our elder brother Jesus and offer praise for answered prayer even before "resurrection morn."

As Jesus did, we must prophesy concerning ourselves and families according to what has been written about us in His Holy Word. *We must choose to walk out of the cadaverous screams of haunting*

rejections and inadequacies and revel in the truth of our right-
eousness in Him!

**"The words of the Lord are pure words: as silver tried in
a furnace of earth, purified seven times."** **Psalm 12:6**

*Calvary became the testing ground for the Word of God, and
the Word proved faithful to perform.*

Jesus walked on the earth totally dependent on the Holy Spirit's
ability to execute the Word of God in His behalf. Jesus tested His
Father's Word and validated the power of the Spirit to move in our
behalf. If no demon could keep Him in death or hell, then how much
more can His Word deliver us from insecurities and condemnation.

If the Father of the universe is satisfied with the finished work
of Christ, how dare we presume less. Let us rejoice that it is more than
sufficient for all of our distresses, and that He hardens us to difficul-
ties. Let us proclaim along with the Scripture in Isaiah 4:2, that "we
are the branch of the Lord, beautiful and glorious, and that our fruit is
excellent and comely."

The Word Transfigures

If obedience to the Word of God determines our self-worth and
confidence as Christian women, then how do we know if we are
being a doer of His Word? What are the signposts that let us know we
are on the path of God's will for our lives? What confirms that we are

in a position where the Holy Spirit can execute godly purposes in our lives?

We must listen to what we are saying.

"For out of the abundance of the heart the mouth speaketh."   **Matthew 12:34**

"For as he thinks in his heart, so is he."

Proverbs 23:7 (Amp)

Our attitudes and opinions determine the length to which God can move in our behalf. How do we become a doer of God's Word? By letting His Holy Spirit discern and judge the intents, thoughts, and purposes of our heart. He wants to be the umpire in our soul, distinguishing between good and evil, and truth and falsehood. The devil is powerless in our life without his cunning device of deception.

"For the word of God is quick, and powerful, and sharper than any two-edged sword, piercing even to the dividing asunder of soul and spirit, and of the joints and marrow, and is a discerner of the thoughts and intents of the heart."   **Hebrews 4:12**

As a young Christian wife and mother, I used to envision myself with a large kitchen sieve over my thought life, allowing the Holy

Spirit to strain my every contemplation, perception, and reasoning. We must allow the Holy Spirit to be the final umpire in our convictions, assessments, and judgments, never letting our thought life veer off the confines of His wisdom.

"Be not conformed to this world: but be ye transformed (3339) by the renewing of your mind, that ye may prove what is that good, and acceptable, and perfect will of God."   **Romans 12:2**

The Greek word used for "transformed" in Romans 12:2 is *metamorphoo* (met-am-or-fo-o 3339). This same Greek word *metamorphoo* is also used In Matthew 17:2 where it is translated *transfigured,* while in Romans 12:2 it is translated *transformed.* There can be an exchanging of these two translations of the same Greek word. We could say it this way, that conforming our mind to the Word of God will "transfigure us."

"Jesus taketh Peter, James, and John his brother, and bringeth them up into a high mountain apart, And was transfigured (3339) before them: and His face did shine as the sun, and his raiment was white as the light."
                    Matthew 17:1,2

It is as we bring our minds captive to the Word of God that our mundane visage will be transfigured into the dazzling brilliance of His

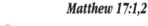

beauty. Our homes and families will be transformed before us, and our face will shine as the noonday sun, as we renew our minds to God's Word and prove His perfect will for our life. The Word of God, big on the inside of us, will transfigure our countenance and situations into His divine radiant glory. Let our hearts cry with the Psalmist:

"Search me, O God, and know my heart: try me, and know my thoughts: and see if there be any wicked way in me, and lead me in the way everlasting."
Psalm 139:23,24

I remember at very stressful times in my young walk with the Lord, I would seek refuge on our back porch late at night and cry out to God in desperation and deep despair. Often He would speak to me, and I would find comfort; but one particular night, He so bluntly stated: *"Jeri, I have done everything I am ever going to do for you."* At first, I was shocked and taken aback that He would speak to me in such a seemingly cold manner, but now I see this was a pivotal point in my life.

He began to minister to me about the finished work of Christ on Calvary, and how I must begin to appropriate His provision by placing His Holy Word on my lips and then my faith would become effective–that I wasn't waiting on Him, but in actuality, He was waiting on me. He was waiting for my faith to become active as I acknowledged every good thing that was in me in Christ. What was in me? Everything that pertained to life and godliness: abundance in marriage, finances, health, ministry, joy, peace, etc. I had resident on the inside of me everything I had been begging for God to give me.

"That the communication of thy faith may become effectual by the acknowledging of every good thing which is in you in Christ Jesus."   **Philemon 6**

Something began to go off on the inside of me, and a new dimension swung open. Surely I was who He said I was, if only I would acquaint myself with what the Scriptures said about me and His will for my life.

Then I began to see a pattern in the life of Jesus. Many well-known Scriptures prophesied His birth, resurrection, etc., but the following Scripture in Isaiah is considered by some scholars as a passage that Jesus meditated on as a young man. We must remember that Jesus wasn't birthed mature and full blown. He had to be taught of the Lord and learn to yield to the voice of the Spirit. He had to desire His Father's presence and quest after His wisdom, just the same as you and I do.

"The Lord hath given me the tongue of the learned, that I should know how to speak a word in season to him that is weary: he wakeneth morning by morning, he wakeneth mine ear to hear as the learned. The Lord God hath opened mine ear, and I was not rebellious, neither turned away back. I gave my back to the smiters, and my

cheeks to them that plucked off the hair: I hid not my face from shame and spitting. For the Lord God will help me; therefore shall I not be confounded: therefore have I set my face like a flint, and I know that I shall not be ashamed."   **Isaiah 50:4-7**

When Jesus walked the earth in His humanity, He had to daily commune with His Father and confess what He had written about Him in the Scriptures to grow up in the things of the Spirit. Jesus as a young boy, had to believe that His Father had given Him the tongue of the learned, and that He would have wisdom to confound the religious men of His day and truth to deliver hungry souls.

He prepared Himself to fulfill His Father's will as He meditated on what the Scriptures had to say about Him. He enabled Himself to hear His Father's voice as He confessed, "His Lord God had opened His ear." *It was only as He believed that He would "not turn back" from the cruel anguish of rejection that He had the strength to endure.* Will God fulfill His will in us in any other way? *No!*

There is only one way, the way Jesus did it. We must agree in faith with God's written Word concerning His purposes, so it can become the living Word, the *zoe* life of God, activated as we place it on our lips. One day the Father opened up His Son's heart and the boy Jesus knew that Isaiah 50:6 was speaking of Him. The Father's will for His crucifixion was revealed to Him, but He did not turn back.

The Bible says that He set His face like flint. *Ladies, we need to be like Jesus!* We need to look into the Scriptures and say, *"That's me!"* We must never turn back from the requirements and call of God that He has spoken. Let us too, "set our face like flint," knowing that He will be there to help and never leave us confounded or ashamed.

Women of the Lord, James speaks of no man being able to tame the tongue, but only the Holy Spirit. As we agree with God that we have been given the tongue of the learned, such *zoe* life will compound on the inside of us, that when the pressures of life attempt to squeeze bitter, raucous remarks from us, only mercy and virtue will flow from our lips as we minister grace to our family.

I have found that the Lord will require many things of us that might not seem agreeable or particularly pleasing. Often we must incur hardships for others, but God always turns the hardships to the good and He promises to never put us to shame and He always offers hope! Let us determine never to turn back from what the Spirit is saying, and guard our hearts that we might be open to what the Spirit has to say.

Countless times the Lord has said, "Jeri, this is what I have for you," and it has been totally contrary to what I had in mind. But as I have submitted to His will and rejoiced in His goodness, there has always been "resurrection morn" and a deeper abiding trust in His perfect ways. He has continually spiraled me into a higher place with Him, which is always fullness of joy.

Chapter 9

Raising
Your Husband

*"We must learn
to switch hats
from that of a mother
to that of a wife."*

I PURPOSELY SELECTED THIS TITLE as a humorous misnomer because who of us at one time or another hasn't tried to "raise our husbands"? But this is a completely erroneous concept, as Scripture never instructs us to "raise our husbands" but instead to esteem and honor them highly. It is our motherly instincts that confuse us here—we often try to apply the training and teaching principles that we should be using with our children.

We misuse this God-given responsibility and unleash all of our zeal on our unsuspecting husbands. We must learn to switch hats from that of a mother to that of a wife.

We must toss our motherly instincts to the wind, as our husband's "lion-ish" nature will not and cannot respond to our attempts to "tame" him to our ways. Our husbands are to furnish our homes with images of strength and indomitability. They are to be our brave men, our mighty heroes. They are to defend against our most powerful and fierce enemies.

Our husband's inherent nature is after that of the "Lion of the Tribe of Judah," after his elder brother, Jesus. Judah, as one of the twelve tribes of Israel, was the first tribe that was allotted its territory in the Promised Land. In over-abundance of their share, the tribe of Judah received fully one-third of the whole land west of the Jordan.

There is an abundance above what we could hope, think or dream that awaits us, when we relinquish the crack of our lion trainer's whip and begin to trust the man that God has placed in our home.

You might be saying that the only aspect of your husband that resembles a lion is his fierceness and cruelty, or on the other hand, perhaps he is passive and reticent, never displaying any boldness of a lion. Whatever the case may be, the Scripture states in Ephesians 5:23, that your husband is the head of you as Christ is the Head of the Church. It also goes on to say in verse 31, that the husband and wife through the mysterious joining in marriage become one—that the *"two shall be one flesh."*

I am fully persuaded that if we as wives could get hold of this one principle, that Satan would forever be defeated in our homes. How does this principle of "two becoming one flesh" practically apply to our lives? It has to do with an awareness of our being "one body" with our husbands. That "one body" has one mouth and one set of eyes and ears. This "one body" is not some monstrous disfigurement, but rather a glorious type of Christ and His Church.

That means if we as wives sit down to partake of a spiritual meal, then our husbands are assimilating that same meal alongside of us, whether they be present in the flesh or not. If one of us hears a rhema Word from the Father, then that same illumination can be imparted to the other by the Spirit of the Living God. What-ever the husband or wife gleans in the Spirit, then their "one body," in which they jointly dwell, reaps the bounty. This is part of the mystery when it comes to the exchange in the Spirit between Christ and the Church and this same impartation can take place in the Spirit between husbands and wives.

I remember when I first got hold of this truth, I was at that stage in my life where I was leaving Christian books around on the coffee table in hopes that my husband would become enticed to pick one up. He rarely did, but to my amazement, just about the time I would laboriously gain some insight into how to improve my walk with the Lord, my husband, almost by osmosis, would catch the same truth. It is amazing to me, that if we as wives will go in and "get the goods," then we will be nourishing our husbands as well as ourselves. There is a partaking that we can do for one another, as we truly are "one flesh."

Joint Heirs Of The Grace Of Life

"...if you forgive the sins of anyone, they are forgiven;
if you retain the sins of anyone, they are retained."
John 20:23 (Amp)

Jesus spoke these words to His disciples immediately after His ascension when He breathed on them to receive the Holy Spirit. One of the most powerful weapons we have as wives is to release our husbands from guilt and condemnation. We are often used as instruments of Satan to hold our husbands in the clutches of sin and bind them to its cursed bondage.

If we retain our husband's sins, then there is a block in the ability of God to move in their behalf. If we forgive their sins, then and only then, is there a release in the Spirit realm for them to perform the will of God for their lives.

"But [realizing that you] are joint heirs of the grace (God's unmerited favor) of life, in order that your prayers may not be hindered and cut off. [Otherwise you cannot pray effectively.]"　　*1 Peter 3:7 (Amp)*

The tormentor lingers around homes seeing what offense he can stir up so that our prayers will be hindered. One concept the Lord so vividly spoke to me was that my husband I are joint heirs of the grace of God. The grace of God is His willingness and ability to move in our behalf. We can never accomplish separately what He has intended to bless us with as "one flesh." We have been eternally yoked together, and there must be a pulling together if we are to go forward in Christ.

If there is a breach in the fellowship with our husbands, then we are not walking in the light as Jesus is in the light. For the Scripture states in 1 John 1:7 that if we are truly walking in the light, then we have unbroken fellowship one with another.

"But if we are living in the light of God's presence, just as Christ does, then we have wonderful fellowship and joy with each other, and the blood of Jesus his Son cleanses us from every sin."　　*1 John 1:7 (TLB)*

I remember a painful time as a young Christian when my husband and I did not seem to be on the same wave length. I would sit out under our willow tree in the country night air and mourn before God, crying out for His delivering hand. The branches would droop so heavily around me, and in the quietness of the evening, I would be canopied in the presence of the Lord. There in the boughs of the willow tree, the Lord would minister to me and satisfy me with Himself.

Even though I was doing all I knew to do to grow up spiritually, attending every seminar of my Bible-belt town and stacking my library to its highest peak, still my tears continued to fall beneath that willow tree as I returned there for the Lord's refreshing. Over that trying season, God graciously met with me under that willow tree and in my isolated times of seeking Him, He solaced me beyond measure. His voice became life to me as He unveiled Himself to my eager heart.

However, there came a time when the willow tree had to be chopped down, for it had withered and died over the hot summer. Even after the cutting down of the tree, I would return to the remaining stump and seek God's face, but the seasons had changed and that time of fellowshipping under the weeping willow limbs was over.

The Holy Spirit spoke to me so clearly, "Jeri, it's time for you to get yourself in a place where you can receive from your husband that comfort and satisfaction which I have been providing. For you to be under his umbrella of blessing, you must believe that I have laid an ax to the root of his 'old nature' and that his 'old man' is dead, just as this willow tree is dead. As you are faithful to see him as I see him, then I will strengthen and anoint him to satisfy you in every way, and I will funnel inexpressible joy down through the favor and protection that he provides."

Then He exhorted me to patiently stay in the place of blessing, that place of honoring and esteeming my husband, and by faith I would inherit the promises. As I was faithful to adore and reverence my husband, then the Lord said He would strengthen and increase our marriage.

I can testify today, that abiding under my husband's covering that God has placed over me, has become the fountain of my life that increasingly overflows in satisfaction and daily pleasure. What a blessing to have God open up our eyes that we might see who our husbands really are. They truly are our satisfiers, our mighty conquerors, our valiant men of God, our Lion of the tribe of Judah. And as we abide under God's place of provision, it is there that He can satisfy and sustain us through that mysterious union of a husband and a wife jointly inheriting the grace of His life.

~≈≈~

Getting To The Place, There

In 1 Kings 17:3, when Elijah was in a time of famine, the Lord spoke to him to get to the brook Cherith where He "commanded the ravens to feed him there." Then when the brook dried up because of a drought, the Lord told him to get to Zarephath where He had commanded a widow woman to sustain him there.

When we serve God, He always has a there for us–a place of provision. When we are faithful to take God at His Word, He will command our husbands to be that place, there for us. He will command them to provide, guard and satisfy our every desire.

"I have seen thy face, as though I had seen the face of God."   *Genesis 33:10*

Jacob spoke these words to Esau, his antagonist and betrayed brother. Esau had threatened to kill Jacob because he felt Jacob had cheated him out of his father's double inheritance. So serious was the breach in their relationship that Jacob had to flee to a distant land to escape the wrath of his brother, Esau.

After many years of separation, God put a plan to reconcile Jacob and Esau into effect. God spoke to Jacob to return to his home-land, but on his way to see Esau, God met with Jacob at a place named Peniel, which in Hebrew means "the face of God."

God knew there had to be preparation in Jacob's heart before he could be restored with his family. That preparation of heart only came from being in the presence of God Almighty.

The Scripture states that Jacob "wrestled a Man" through the night, but when daybreak came, Jacob declared, "I have seen God face to face." In other words, Jacob has wrestled with God that night until he began to see things the way God did.

It was only after his encounter with God and complete sub-mission to Him that Jacob was able to reunite with Esau, declaring that when he saw Esau's face it was if he had seen the face of God.

What a total miracle! Esau, the brother that had once manhunted Jacob, had now become "like the face of God."

It was then that I began to understand all those years of seeking under the willow tree. God was preparing my heart as He faithfully met me face to face, that I might emerge at daybreak saying, "When I see the face of my husband, surely I've seen the face of God."

Ladies, as we are faithful to seek God's presence, then He will clear our vision to behold the "face of God" in our husbands. And like Jacob, God will rename us Israel, "a prince of God, that has power with God and man and has won success." (Genesis 32:28)

"Whose adorning let it not be that outward adorning of plaiting the hair, and of wearing of gold, or of putting on of apparel; But let it be the hidden man of the heart, in that which is not corruptible, even the ornament of a meek and quiet spirit, which is in the sight of God of great price."　　　*1 Peter 3:3,4*

"It was thus that Sarah obeyed Abraham [following his guidance and acknowledging his headship over her by] calling him lord (master, leader, authority). And you are now her true daughters if you do right and let nothing terrify you [not giving way to hysterical fears or letting anxieties unnerve you]."　　　*1 Peter 3:6 (Amp)*

This Scripture speaks of a wife's beauty and charm being that of the hidden man of the heart and not of her outward appearance. It speaks of an inward adorning of the heart which is incorruptible and unfading, that is gentle and peaceful and not anxious.

Then in verse 6, it speaks of Sarah following Abraham's guidance and calling him lord. It states that we can be her daughters if we do right and let nothing terrify us or unnerve us. We are encouraged not to give way to hysterical fears.

How do we as women get to the place, *there,* where God commands things in times of famine to nourish us, and things in the time of drought to sustain us? How do we make it through the hard times of a marriage commitment?

We must get to the place, there, which for godly wives is the submission of our souls to highly esteem and praise our husbands. We must continue along consistently abiding in peace and composure, knowing that we are in route to the place, there.

When anxieties come along to unnerve us, we must rebuke hysterical fears and, along with Sarah, call our men lord and confidently abide there, knowing it is there that the Lord will command blessings.

Adorning The Hidden Man Of The Heart

We have seen how we can adorn the hidden man of our heart by putting on a gentle, peaceful, submissive spirit as readily as we would adorn ourselves with costly jewels. We are encouraged not to merely adorn our outward appearances with hairdos and wardrobes, but we are to lavish the inward man of our heart with incorruptible ornaments that never fade.

It goes on in verse five to speak of holy women in the old times who trusted God, and adorned themselves, being in subjection to their husbands. I want to emphasize, *the way we adorn the hidden man of our heart is be in subjection to our husbands.*

"For after this manner in the old time the holy women also, who trusted (1679) **in God, adorned themselves, being in subjection unto their own husbands."**

1 Peter 3:5

The word "trusted" is the Greek word *elpizo* (el·pid´·zo 1679) from 1680 which means *to hope or wait for salvation with joy; to anticipate with pleasure and confidence; to hope to receive something from God.* *

There is a preciousness in the sight of God when we submit to our husbands. When we submit to our husbands, we are showing our trust in God. When we trust God, we will be in submission to our husbands.

God values the maturity involved in submission, as we anticipate with pleasure God's faithfulness to intervene in our behalf—to command the blessings in our behalf.

Submission is the place, "there," where we will always inherit a blessing.

* *Thayer.*

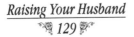

Often that blessing is an enriched romance in the "lions' den." The reverencing and honoring of our husbands is the ultimate "beauty treatment" that allures our husbands to stand up and take notice of our "fascinating good looks."

What is this power to entice or attract our husband's affections? It is the adorning of the hidden man of our heart by deferring to our husbands and trusting God.

"...let the wife see that she respects and reverences her husband [that she notices him, regards him, honors him, prefers him, venerates, and esteems him; and that she defers to him, praises him, and loves and admires him exceedingly]."　　　　*Ephesians 5:33 (Amp)*

I remember the time in my life when I looked up the word "venerate" in the dictionary because I was attempting to obey this Scripture and did not have a clear understanding of its meaning. I am blessed to have a reprint of Noah Webster's original dictionary, first published in 1828.* Noah Webster was a devoted Christian who was fluent in ten languages and spent over 60 years solitarily writing by hand the dictionary that God had called him to write.

One cannot read his definitions without sensing the Holy Spirit's capture of the scriptural essence of words for all posterity to treasure. Webster's legacy to mankind shows the meticulous care God takes to see that we walk in the full impact of His Word.

* *Noah Webster's First Edition of an American Dictionary of the English Language.*

Don't you just love the thoroughness of God and His unrelenting quest over the ages to conform us to His image? Needless to say, I was convicted of my deep need to expand my conception of submission when I read Webster's definition of "veneration."

> **veneration:** *(noun)* The highest degree of respect and reverence; respect mingled with some degree of awe; a feeling or sentiment excited by the dignity and superiority of a person, or by the sacredness of his character; secret awe for one that moves above us in illustrious virtue.

Ladies, God is requiring that we stand in wonder and awe of our husbands' sacred character and that our feelings be excited by their dignity and illustrious virtue. There is a "place" that we can come into, like Sarah, where we call our husbands lord and inherit the blessings.

These admonitions to highly esteem our husbands have literally been life to me whenever I have become disgruntled with my marriage. The Lord consistently returns my heart and mind to these precious instructions.

Oh, Father, may we be found faithful when we stand before Your throne. May we implicitly perform Your Holy Word and be blessed with the romance that only comes from honoring our husbands in the "lions' den."

"For the Lord hath created a new thing in the earth, A woman shall compass (5437) a man." *Jeremiah 31:22*

The Hebrew word for compass is *câbab* (saw-bab´ 5437). It is a primitive root meaning to revolve, *surround* or *border*...be about on every side...*cause to come about...compass*...round; *to prepare a means of attaining.* *

Webster's dictionary traces the origin of the word "compass" to the Spanish and Portuguese language where its original connotation was "a stepping together" or a "beating of time in music."

We as women of God, are to agree with His Word, that we are this "new thing" that He has created. ** That we are this woman who will surround and border our man with the testimonies of the Lord, and we will prepare a means for our husbands to attain all that God has prophesied concerning them. That we will "step together" harmoniously down the path for our life, synchronized by the beat of God's Holy Spirit.

"And blessed is she that believed: for there shall be a performance of those things which were told her from the Lord."   **Luke 1:45**

This prophetic word still applies to women of God today who dare to believe Him and take Him at His Word. Let us exceedingly rejoice together that there will be a performance of those things which have been told to us by the Lord.

---

* The New Brown-Driver-Briggs-Gesenius Hebrew and English Lexicon.
** Webster, 1828 version.

Let us confess together, that we call those things which be not as though they were—who against hope we believe in hope—we consider not our own flesh—we stagger not at the promise of God through unbelief; but we are strong in faith giving glory to God; being fully persuaded that what He has promised, He is well able also to perform. (Romans 4:17-21)

After the age of child-bearing, Sarah "considered her own flesh" when she suggested that her husband lie with her maid Hagar to conceive a descendant to establish God's promises in their lives. It was a well-intentioned endeavor, but totally in the flesh and not prompted by the Spirit of God.

It wasn't until she stopped "considering her own flesh" that Isaac was birthed in her barren womb according to the Word of the Lord.

God is a master at working in dead, infertile situations that He supernaturally impregnates by His Spirit. But He only works when our flesh is dead and we are alive in Him. Notice God didn't start performing His Word in Sarah's life until her womb was dead, which was a type of her fleshly, carnal endeavors to produce God's will in her own strength. He wants us totally dependent upon His Spirit, and it is not until we die to the ways of our flesh that His Spirit will move in our behalf.

God did not impregnate Sarah until her flesh was "dead."

The Scriptures state that "no flesh will touch His glory." God will not fulfill His promises until we reckon our "old nature" crucified with Christ and walk in His newness of life in the Spirit.

We must become "dead" to the ways of our fleshly nature before God's will comes to fruition in our lives. We must be totally dependent on His Spirit and His Spirit alone. We must learn to trust in the Spirit's willingness and ability to move in behalf of our mates.

To access the promises of God, we must go into the tent like Sarah finally did and act like God's Word is true. We are only sending "Hagar maids" into our husband's tent when we use the arm of flesh to change our husbands. Scolding, pouting, berating, and tantrums are "Hagar maids" that will not produce the child of promise, but only the child of flesh, Ishmael.

Still to this day, we are reaping the havoc of Ishmael, the fleshly child of Hagar and Isaac. Ishmael, the progenitor of the Arab people, still harasses the fulfillment of God's promises in the earth.

Our "old nature's" response to our husbands will hinder the promises of God in our lives. We will bring havoc into our lives when we respond in our lower nature's selfish ways and "consider the way of our flesh." Ladies, we have all become desperate and tried to make things happen by our own efforts, but let's use Sarah as our example– it simply doesn't work! We must die to petty accusations against our husbands, innuendoes of self-pity, subtle pressure tactics, and prideful fantasies. Screaming doubts of the flesh must be silenced in the presence of God's Word.

The biblical meaning for "remember" is to "mention." According to Scripture, we haven't remembered something until we have recalled it or mentioned it. Oftentimes as wives, we take a perfect night and annihilate it with words we don't really mean, and then we desperately try to retrieve our illusive romance as it fades into a barrage of hurts. We desolate our present happiness by mentioning and recalling all the mishaps of our past.

In Hebrews 11:15, it speaks of the Israelites having had an opportunity to return had they been mindful of the country from where they came, but they desired a better country, a heavenly city. It is the same with our husbands, if we continually drag up the past and communicate our discontent, we will cause those things to be repeated in our relationship and endlessly cycle in despair. Or, we can press forward to a heavenly marriage, a better place where we "mention" what God has promised us.

When my husband and I were first married, we were not saved. When we did turn to the Lord, there were years of entanglements to unwind from, and with my degree in psychology, I figured we needed to talk things through. Feelings were unearthed that neither one of us needed to remember and the web of heartache wound tighter than ever as our marriage lay lifeless in the stranglehold of the past.

The Lord so brilliantly instructed me after our "talking things through" had so miserably failed, to never say anything about my husband that I didn't want to come to pass: not to question him as to why he would do such and such, or enumerate things that needed to change. He told me that when my husband came home in the evening, I was to treat him as if Jesus Christ had just walked through the door.

The Lord focused my attention upon all the areas in which I personally could improve. He reminded me that Eve was taken out of Adam's rib and that ribs protect the heart from injury or damage. He encouraged me to be that "rib" for my husband–that helpmate that He had sovereignly set alongside my husband to support and believe in at all costs. He said if I would be the helpmate that my husband needed, then my husband would satisfy my every heart's desire.

The Lord reminded me that if I was to inherit a blessing myself, then I must first bless my husband.

"Never return evil for evil or insult for insult (scolding, tongue-lashing, berating) but on the contrary blessing [praying for their welfare, happiness and protection, and truly pitying and loving them]. For know that to this you have been called, that you may yourselves inherit a blessing [from God]." 1 Peter 3:9 (Amp)

This Scripture was actually written to husbands concerning their wives, but I believe it is a reciprocal calling for husbands and wives that we bless one another so that we ourselves might inherit a blessing from God.

The Wrong Tree

Eve chose to eat of the wrong tree. She could have eaten of the tree of life, but instead she chose to partake of the tree of the knowledge of good and evil. The tree of knowledge of good and evil can be a type of a critical mindset, where we set ourselves up as judges who judge according to the seeing of the eye and hearing of the ear.

I think Eve exemplifies what every woman is vulnerable to when we doubt and question with Eve, "Hath God really said?" We will continually be harassed and tempted when we entertain the thought, "Maybe so, maybe not."

We must cease from wavering and begin to reign in the absolute immutable authority of His Word. Should we believe crafty lies and doubt what God has spoken to us, then we too partake of the tree of judgment and begin to align ourselves with the accuser of the brethren, Satan.

I believe when Eve partook of the fruit that her eyes opened to both her frailties and Adam's as well. All their weaknesses became bigger than God Himself and suddenly they were ashamed of themselves and one another.

According to the devil's standards, we and our spouses always come short of the glory of God. We can never measure up. But Jesus came to break the curse of the law, which is falling short of the glory of God, and in Christ we measure up.

We must be visionaries and astute enough in the Scriptures to allow His Word to color our view of one another.

"Wherefore henceforth know we no man after the flesh... Therefore if any man be in Christ, he is a new creature: old things are passed away; behold, all things are become new." **2 Corinthians 5:16,17**

"So stop evaluating Christians by what the world thinks about them or by what they seem to be like on the outside. Once I mistakenly thought of Christ that way, merely as a human being like myself. How differently I feel now! When someone becomes a Christian he becomes a brand new person inside. He is not the same any more. A new life has begun!"

2 Corinthians 5:16,17 (TLB)

Ladies, let's let that new life begin in our husbands and agree with God. One connotation of the word judge is "to critically watch." Why are we instructed not to judge? Because verse 17 says, "old things have passed away and all things have become new." There was a time in my life that God convicted me of being a "Ham." What do I mean by that? Let me show you the Scripture He ministered to me.

"Noah, a man of the soil, proceeded to plant a vineyard. When he drank some of its wine, he became drunk and lay uncovered inside his tent. Ham, the father of Canaan, saw his father's nakedness and told his two brothers outside. But Shem and Japheth took a garment and laid it across their shoulders; then they walked in backward and covered their father's nakedness.

Their faces were turned the other way so that they would not see their father's nakedness."

Genesis 9:20-23 (NIV)

Notice the two different responses of the brothers. One *"saw and told"* and the others *"covered and refused to see."* How easy it is to see what our husbands are doing wrong and then tell them. It is quite another to refuse to see them in the natural and view them only by spiritual truths and cover them by the blood of Jesus, to hold our tongue and allow the Spirit to move.

Ham was the progenitor of the Hamitic people who peopled Africa and became the nation of Egypt *which held God's people in bondage and slavery.* Shem, on the other hand, was the progenitor of Abram and Isaac. In Genesis l2:2 God promises to bless Abram and make him a great nation. Not only does He promise to bless him but make him a blessing in which all the families of the earth will be blessed.

It is true that we are of the seed of Abraham, and that God intends to use our families to bless all the families of the earth, but we must align our hearts with the Abrahamic heart of mercy. I think God is requiring unique responses in Christian homes that have learned of Him.

Are we going to hold God's people in bondage by our critical eye, or will we choose to be "earth blessers"? Will we refuse to dwell on the sin, and instead choose to meet the needs? If we truly intend to be His "earth blessers," then we must respond in mercy, one to another.

Chapter 10

The Test

"Continue to stand,
remembering that
He is faithful
to complete what
He has begun."

*T*HE GREEK WORD "TRIAL," *dokimion* (dok·im´·ee·on 1383) appears only two times in the New Testament, yet it contains a very powerful concept. It means *a testing for genuineness and trustworthiness.* * Its meaning is drawn from metallurgical chemistry where metal is melted in a crucible to test its genuineness and remove any impurities. Metal not submitted to this process is a relatively worthless chunk of ore.

"Wherein ye greatly rejoice, though now for a season, if need be, ye are in heaviness through manifold temptations: That the trial (1383) of your faith, being much more precious than of gold that perisheth, though it be tried with fire, might be found unto praise and honour and glory at the appearing of Jesus Christ."   *1 Peter 1:6,7*

"My brethren, count it all joy, when ye fall into divers temptations; Knowing this, that the trying (1383) of your faith worketh patience. But let patience have her perfect work, that ye may be perfect and entire, wanting nothing."   *James 1:2-4*

As Christian women who have purposed to be "altogether given to God," we can expect to have our faith tested as to its gen-

* Thayer, Vine.

uineness. He will require that we prove our trustworthiness to abide in "His presence," no matter what. It is this "trying of our faith" that allows us to evaluate the purity and depth of our commitment to His ways. For it is the pure in heart that will see God, and only as we are purged by His Holy Spirit will our hearts visibly focus upon His holiness.

A "test" we face as wives and mothers often comes in the form of delayed answer to prayer, beyond the point where it seems we can hold on. Will we become bitter and ugly during these dry spells, cutting off the flow of "His presence"?

It is when we persevere continued stretches of delay beyond human tolerance, that we enter into the "trying of our faith." At this point we can begin to rejoice, for we know God is getting ready to approve our faith and stamp it "endorsed and tested." Along with this validation, comes His still small voice: "Ask what you will, daughter, for you have remained faithful and pure, and I deem you empowered."

Oh, what a sweet hour of revenge against the pressures that struck our composure and relentlessly buffeted our hopes. Oh, what a precious thing, when our faith redounds praise, honor and glory to His name; when our faith rises and swells as waves of pleasure and satisfaction before His face. As we "pass the test" and prove our faith to be genuine, we flood the earth's shores with abundant waves and drive back every evil.

Let's never give up; let's be relentless in our charge to "walk within our house with The Perfect Heart." No matter at what age or level of maturity we and our families are, let us not lose heart or courage, but let us tenaciously rejoice in our test of faith. Let us, having done all to stand, continue to stand, remembering that He is faithful to complete what He has begun.

There will be testings to arouse us out of spiritual sleep–to wake us from the sluggish worldly mindset–to see if we will yield to His spiritual awakening. He not only wants us to separate from sin, but furthermore, make a distinction between that which is merely good and that which is holy. Daily we are presented with low and high choices of living.

He is calling us up to a higher place of life where the acceptable becomes excellent, where concern becomes impassioned zealousness and good intentions resolve into empowered holy actions. He desires that we become flushed with the fiery glow from His countenance and exhilarated with "His presence."

It is no longer just a matter of separating ourselves from evil, but fully submitting our hearts to the sanctification of the Holy Spirit.

He wants to crush our satisfaction with mere good and press us into His holiness.

He attentively stands in the heavenlies with His host of warring angels, ready to hearken to the voice of genuine hearts, "altogether given to Him."

"...a woman named Martha received and welcomed Him into her house. And she had a sister named Mary, who seated herself at the Lord's feet and was listening to His teaching. But Martha [overly occupied and too busy] was distracted with much serving...the Lord replied...

Martha, Martha, you are anxious and troubled about many things; There is need of only one or but a few things. Mary has chosen the good portion [that which is to her advantage], which shall not be taken away from her."   *Luke 10:38-42 (Amp)*

Let's be like Mary and seat ourselves at our Lord's feet, choosing the good portion that will not be taken away. Blessings come full circle, and as we dare to depart from the normalcy of mediocre marriages and ordinary motherhood, God will greatly recompense those of us who venture to learn of Him and trust His Word—prostrating ourselves before the beauty of His holiness at the cost of all else.

"The words of the Lord are pure words; as silver tried in a furnace of earth, purified seven times." Psalm 12:6

Our precious Lord Jesus' words were tested and tried and proven genuine in the furnace of Calvary.

Jesus' words were proved genuine to the point of pouring out His own blood and faithful to lift Him from the clutches of hell. There was a time in the Garden of Gethsemane when Jesus' disciples fell asleep leaving Him abandoned in agony. The word "Gethsemane" means an "oil press" (1068). *He was crushed and pressed of His life that we might be anointed to "pass the test."*

We must be faithful to allow God to approve our faith, so that He can openly reward us with the fruit of His harvest. Let's not be weary in well-doing, but let us press toward the mark of the high calling in Christ Jesus. Let us learn to feed off the life of God that He has deposited within our families and abound toward one another in love.

Say together with me, "I will walk within my house with a perfect heart."

Scripture
Library

☙ *Children* ❧

Confess the following with faith in the integrity of God's Word, that it will prosper that to which it is sent.

My children hear the instruction of their father and forsake not the teachings of their mother.   Proverbs 1:8,9

Because my children get Wisdom (the Word of God), and do not forsake her, she preserves them. Because they love Wisdom, she shall keep them. Because they exalt Wisdom, she will exalt them. Because they hold her fast, she will lead them to great honor. She will place a beautiful crown upon their head, because they embrace her.   Proverbs 4:5-9

My children listen carefully to what the Spirit is saying, and keep His thoughts ever in their minds, letting them penetrate deep within their hearts. God's Words become real life to them and radiant health. Above all else, they guard diligently the issues of their hearts and their affections (their zealous attachment toward things that hold excitement). Their affections are turned toward God and influence the consequences of their life for good.   Proverbs 4:20-24

My sons are as vigorous plants even grown up large in their youth; my daughters are as corner pillars, polished after the similitude of a palace.   Psalm 144:12

Because my children and I go yonder and worship, we will come again, triumphing over every challenge.   Genesis 22:5

My children do not say they are only a youth; for they go to all whom You send them and speak whatever You command them.   Jeremiah 1:6

God sends an angel before my family to keep them in the way, and to bring them into the place that God has prepared.   Exodus 23:20

My children have the same spirit as Caleb, who says, "Let us go up at once and possess it; we are well able to conquer it." As God's servant, Caleb, they do not follow the crowd but have a different kind of spirit who fully follows God. Therefore, God brings them into the land, and they possess His promises.   Numbers 13:30 & 14:24

Because I do not allow my children to grumble and complain, they are pleasing to the Lord.   Numbers 11:1

Just as young Solomon sought You for wisdom, they inquire of You as more precious than fine silver or gold, and You give them an understanding heart to discern between good and evil and enable

them to bless the nations. Because they seek Your wisdom first, You add to them riches, honor and a long life. 1 Kings 3:7,8

I thank You, Lord, that like Elisha's servant, You open the eyes of my children to see and behold the mountains full of Your warring horsemen and chariots of fire round about them. They will not be afraid of the seemingly insurmountable odds in this world, but they trust in You, the "Horseman of Israel." 2 Kings 6:7

Because my children obey and serve You, they will spend their days in prosperity and their years in pleasures. Job 36:11

My children hide Your Word in their heart that they might not sin against You. Psalm 119:11

My children are my inheritance from the Lord, and God's reward to me. Psalm 127:3

Because I correct my children, they give me rest and bring delight to my soul. Proverbs 29:17

My children are redeemed of the Lord. The Lord has bought them back from the clutches of darkness, and they say so with a grateful heart and speak out in thankful praises. Psalm 107:2

My children have great peace because they love Your Word; nothing shall offend them or make them stumble.　　　*Psalms 119:165*

My children choose to bless You with their soul; all that is within them blesses Your holy name. I teach them to speak to their mind, to command their mind, to grab the attention of their mind and "forget not Your benefits." They bless You by remembering all Your benefits–then You satisfy them with good things.　　　*Psalm 103*

You make my children ministers (those who attend as a worshipper) as a flaming fire.　　　*Psalm 104:4*

Because I teach my children to walk uprightly, You give them grace and glory, and no good thing will You withhold from them.

Psalm 84:11

I usher my children into Your sanctuary where they look upon You and see Your power and glory. You evidence Yourself by peace and joy in their hearts.　　　*Psalm 63:2*

My children cleanse their way by taking heed according to Your Word.　　　*Psalm 119:9*

✑ Family ✑

We teach our children to meditate on Scripture as Jesus did as a boy. Oh, how they love Your Word! It is their meditation all the day. Through your commandments, You make them wiser than their enemies; for Your words are ever before them.
Psalm 119:97,98

I am a fruitful vine by the side of our home, and our children are like olive plants round about our table.   *Psalm 128:3*

Our souls long, yes even faint for the courts of the Lord; our hearts and flesh cry out for the living God. One day in Your courts is better than a thousand anywhere else. Psalm 84:2,10

Because we are slow to anger, we are better than the mighty, and when we rule our own spirit, we are better than he who takes a city.

Proverbs 16:32

Our family's gifts make room for us and bring us before great men.

Proverbs 18:16

Many plans are in our mind, but it is only the Lord's purpose for us that will stand.   *Proverbs 19:21*

When our ways please the Lord, He makes even our enemies to be at peace with us.   Proverbs 16:7

The blessing of the Lord makes us rich, and He adds no sorrow with it.   Proverbs 10:22

His fruit is better than gold, yes, than refined gold, and His increase than choice silver.   Proverbs 8:19

When we are humble and reverently worship the Lord, He rewards us with riches, honor, and long life.   Proverbs 22:4

We will build our house on godly wisdom and by understanding we will establish it. By knowledge are the rooms of our home filled with all precious and pleasant riches.
Proverbs 24:3,4

Father, I thank You that You have given us a spirit of wisdom and revelation in the deep, intimate knowledge of You—that we are hungering to know You better. I thank You that the eyes of our hearts are flooded with light to see the hope You have called us to and the riches of Your glorious inheritance. We thank You that we increasingly understand the exceeding greatness of Your power that

works in us when we believe. It is the same mighty power which You used to raise Christ from the dead and seat Him at Your own right hand in heaven.   *Ephesians 1:17-23*

We are satisfied with good by the fruit of our mouth and the works of our hands shall come back to us.   *Proverbs 12:14*

Because we are in fellowship with You, our path shines brighter and brighter as the noonday sun. Each morning gives way to Your splendor as we walk in the light of Your favor.   *Proverbs 4:18*

We roll our works upon You, Lord! We commit and trust each and every endeavor wholly into Your hands. Then You cause our thoughts to become agreeable to Your will and establish our plans to succeed.   *Proverbs 16:3*

We open our mouths with godly wisdom, and in our tongue is the law of lovingkindness.   *Proverbs 31:26*

Because we have the heart of the wise, we teach our mouths and add learning to our lips.   *Proverbs 16:23*

Because we have a glad heart, we will have a continual feast regardless of circumstances.   *Proverbs 15:15*

The Lord God gives us the tongue of the learned, so that we can know how to speak a word in season to those who are weary. He wakens us morning by morning, He wakens our ears to hear as the learned. The Lord has opened our ears, and we are not rebellious nor turn back.   *Isaiah 50:4,5*

You make us exceedingly glad with the joy of Your presence. Your presence is sufficient for us.   *Psalm 21:6*

Whatever our task, we do it heartily unto You, Lord, and not unto men. You make us exceedingly glad with the joy that comes from being in Your presence.   *Colossians 3:23*

Our hearts stand in awe of Your Word.   *Psalm 119:161*

My feet hold closely to Your paths and the tracks of the One Who has gone before me. My feet do not slip.   *Psalm 17:5*

The Lord has heard my supplication and received my prayer.
Psalm 6:9

My gentle tongue (with its healing power) is a tree of life, but if
I'm willfully contrary, I break down my family's spirits.
Proverbs 15:4

My ears shall hear a word behind me saying, this is the way,
walk in it, when I turn to the right hand and when I turn to the
left.   Isaiah 30:21

I will not be afraid, ashamed, confused or depressed! You will
cause me to forget the shame of my youth, and I will not
remember the sorrow of my former life when I was without You.
For now You are My maker and husband, the Lord of hosts; and
my Redeemer, the Holy One of Israel.   Isaiah 54:4,5

Because I intimately know You, God, You will cause me to
prove myself strong and stand firm, and do great exploits for
You.   Daniel 11:32

Because I am wise, I shall shine as the brightness of the firmament   *Daniel 12:3*

Out of the abundance of my heart, my mouth speaks. What's in my heart determines my speech. As I meditate on Your Holy Word, I will say what You say.   *Matthew 12:34*

When I have a wilderness experience, like Jesus, I will speak the Word and return in the power of God's Spirit.   *Luke 4:14*

Because I believe, I will see the glory of God.   *John 11:40*

I no longer judge any man after the flesh, that is according to what I see with my eyes and hear with my ears, but I see them according to what the Word of God says about them.   *John 8:15*

When I speak God's Word, His Spirit and life are released.   *John 6:63*

When the ruler of this world, Satan, comes, he finds nothing of himself in me. There is no hook that he can put in my flesh, for I reckon my old man dead and I am a new creation alive in Christ.

John 14:30

I see You, Lord, always before me. Because You are at my right hand, I will not be shaken; therefore my heart rejoices and my tongue is glad; You make known to me the paths of my life, and You fill me with joy in Your presence. Acts 2:25-28

I am more blessed when I give than when I receive. Acts 20:35

I present my body a living sacrifice, holy acceptable unto God, which is my reasonable service. I am not conformed to this world; but I am transformed by the renewing of my mind, that I may prove what is the good, acceptable, and perfect will of God.

Romans 12:1,2

My faith increases as I hear and continue to hear the rhema Word (that particular Scripture the Holy Spirit speaks to my heart) released from my lips. Romans 10:17

The love of God has been shed abroad in my heart by the Holy Spirit, and now I am empowered to love only as the Holy Spirit can.

Romans 5:5

I stagger not at the promise of God through unbelief; but I am strong in faith, giving glory to God. I am fully persuaded that what He has promised, He is able also to perform. Romans 4:20

I put on the Lord Jesus Christ and make no provision for the flesh, to fulfill its lusts.   Romans 13:14

I know that if He did not withhold or spare even His own Son but gave Him up for me, then He will also freely and graciously give me all other things.   Romans 8:32

Righteousness, peace and joy in the Holy Ghost are signposts that I am in the presence of God. I guard and keep these with utmost diligence.   Romans 14:17

I call those things which be not as though they were, and against hope I still believe in hope.   Romans 4:17,18

I suffer long and am kind; I am not envious; do not parade myself haughtily, I am not puffed up; do not behave rudely, do not seek my own interests, am not easily provoked. I think no evil, I do not rejoice in iniquity but rejoice with the truth; I bear all things, believe all things, hope all things, endure all things. My love never fails.

1 Corinthians 13:4-8

*Like a boxer, I buffet my body—handle it roughly—discipline it—
subdue it—and bring it under subjection to my spirit.*

1 Corinthians 9:27

*My light afflictions are for but a moment, and they work for me
an exceeding, eternal weight of glory. I look not at the things
which are seen, but at the things which are not seen; for the
things which are seen are temporal, but the things which are
not seen are eternal.* *2 Corinthians 4:17,18*

*I walk by faith and not by sight—I'm not despondent when
circumstances appear contrary to the Word of God, but my
hope and trust are in His immutable Word that changes things.*

2 Corinthians 5:7

*God is able to make all grace (favor in His presence) abound
toward me, always having all sufficiency in all things, having
an abundance for every good work.* *2 Corinthians 9:8*

*When the Holy Spirit controls my life, He will produce this kind
of fruit in me; love, joy, peace, patience, kindness, goodness,
faithfulness, gentleness, and self-control. When I am living and
moving in the Holy Spirit, there is no law that can bring a
charge against me.* *Galatians 5:22,23*

Father, I thank You that when I speak to myself in psalms, and hymns and spiritual songs, and sing and make melody in my heart to You, Lord, then You fill me with Your Spirit.   Ephesians 5:18,19

God, You are all the while effectually at work in me, energizing and creating in me the power and desire both to will and to work for Your good pleasure, satisfaction, and delight.   Philippians 2:13

I am learning in whatsoever state I am in, to be independent of circumstances.   Philippians 4:11

Father, I thank You that You fill me with the knowledge of Your will in all wisdom and spiritual understanding. I am walking worthy of You and pleasing in everything. I am fruitful in every good work and increasing in the knowledge of You. Colossians 1:9-14

Whatever I do in word or deed, I do it heartily unto You, Lord, and not unto men.   Colossians 3:23

I continually thank You, God, that I have received Your Word and that it is effectually working in me because I believe.
1 Thessalonians 2:13

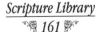

In everything I give thanks, for this is God's will.

1 Thessalonians 5:18

When I meditate upon Your Word and give myself wholly to it, then my profiting appears to all. Meditation on Your Holy Word is the matrix of my creativity.   *1 Timothy 4:15*

I come boldly to Your throne of grace that I might receive mercy and find grace to help in my time of need.   *Hebrews 4:16*

I enter into Your presence every time when I mix my faith with Your finished work on Calvary and what Your shed blood has done for me.

Hebrews 10:19

Seeing that You are My great High Priest Who has passed into the heavenlies, I hold fast to my confession of faith without wavering that we two might be in agreement and that You perform Your Word.

Hebrews 4:14

Father, I thank You that You are upholding all things that concern me by the Word of Your power.   *Hebrews 1:3*

I know that without faith it is impossible to please You; and that when I come to You, I must believe that You are, and that You reward me when I diligently seek and inquire of You. Hebrews 11:6

I am a doer of Your Word and not a hearer only. For if I am a hearer only, I deceive myself. If I only look in the mirror of Your Word and then walk away, I will forget what I really look like or who I am in Christ.   *James 1:22-24*

When I submit myself to You and resist the devil, he will flee from me!   *James 4:7*

I not only love in word or tongue, but in deed and truth.
1 John 3:18

I overcome the devil when I give voice to the blood of Christ in the earth and speak prophetically concerning what the Word of God has to say about my family.   *Revelation 12:11*

My prayers are as arrows in the heart of the King's enemies.
Psalm 45:5

He has given me everything that pertains to life and godliness through full and personal knowledge of Him.   *2 Peter 1:3*

I am the branch of the Lord, beautiful and glorious, and my fruit is excellent and lovely.   *Isaiah 4:2*

I continually behold Your face in righteousness, and I am fully satisfied when I awake to behold You. I have sweet communion with You and find contentment knowing all is well between us.
    Psalm 17:15

When I take refuge and put my trust in You, I can rejoice, knowing that You make a covering over me and defend me. You surround me with a shield of pleasure and favor.   *Psalm 5:11,12*

You sow light in my pathway, and I have irrepressible joy when I am consciously aware of Your favor and protection.   *Psalm 97:11*

 *Husbands*

My husband and I are joint heirs of the grace of life, and because we honor one another, our prayers are not hindered.   *1 Peter 3:7*

My husband is filled with the knowledge of Your will in all spiritual wisdom and understanding.   *Colossians 1:9*

I compass round my husband on every side with the Word of God. I prepare a means for him to fulfill God's plans and cause God's purposes to come about in his life.   *Jeremiah 31:22*

I respect, yield to, revere, honor, esteem, adore, appreciate, prize, admire, praise, deeply love, and enjoy my husband. I stand in awe of his sacred character and my feelings are excited by his dignity and illustrious virtue.   *1 Peter 3:2 (Amp)*

My husband and I are of the same mind, united in Spirit, loving each other with compassionate, tender hearts.   *1 Peter 3:8*

We never return insult for insult or evil for evil. We do not scold or belittle one another, but we pray for each other's welfare that we might inherit a blessing.   *1 Peter 3:9*

Like Sarah, I call my husband lord and do not give way to hysterical fears or anxieties that could unnerve me.   *1 Peter 3:6*

When I am submitted to my husband, I am trusting in God.

1 Peter 3:5

I clothe myself with love for my husband. I put on gentleness, long-suffering and good temper as a garment. I readily pardon and forgive him. We are enfolded with bonds of perfectness and rest together in harmony. Peace is ruling in our hearts as umpire, settling all questions that arise. I am thankful and appreciative of him.

Colossians 3:12-15

My husband and I lean our entire personalities on God in absolute trust and confidence in His power, wisdom and goodness.

Proverbs 2:7

We shun youthful lusts and pursue righteousness and virtuous living that conforms to the will of God in thought, word and deed. We refuse to have unedifying stupid quarrels that breed strife. Instead we are kind, mild-tempered, courteous and forbearing. *2 Timothy 2:22-24*

We hear the voice of God because we do not harden our hearts in the time of testings. *Hebrews 3:15*

We draw near God's throne of grace in our time of need and appropriate help comes just when we need it. Hebrews 4:16

We cannot curse each other who are made in God's likeness and with the same mouth bless the Lord. We are pure fountains that only spring forth sweet water and not bitter. James 3:9-11

We submit ourselves to God, stand firm against the devil, resist him and he flees from us. We draw close to God and He comes close to us. James 4:7,8

We confess our faults and offenses one to another, praying for one another that we might be healed and restored. Our fervent prayers avail much and have tremendous power because we are in right standing with God. James 5:16

Above all, we have intense and unfailing love for one another. This great love covers a multitude of sins as we forgive and disregard each other's offenses. 1 Peter 4:8

God's love for my husband has been poured out in my heart by the Holy Spirit. The Holy Spirit quickens and gives life to our marriage. Romans 5:5

My husband and I still bring forth fruit in our old age and we are full of spiritual vitality. We are rich in the verdure of trust, love and contentment. We are living memorials to show that You are faithful to Your promises. Psalm 92:14,15 (Amp)

From
The Author

*T*hought you might enjoy a grown-up picture of my family to go along with all the stories that took place in the process. May we stand as a living testimony to the goodness of God, and that you too can triumph over challenges that confront aspiring hearts. I recently finished home schooling our two daughters, Amy and Grace, and am presently ministering in my local church.

"He who did not withhold or spare [even] His own Son but gave Him up for us all, will He not also with Him freely and graciously give us all [other] things?"
Romans 8:32 (Amp)

My dear friend, whatever need you might have, call upon the wonderful name of Jesus and let Him begin to create in you that perfect heart out of which all blessings flow.

I would love to hear from you and welcome your correspondence or prayer requests.

Jeri

To contact the author, please write or call:
Jeri Williams Ministries
9921 Carmel Mountain Road · San Diego, CA 92129 · 619-484-7184

*About
The Author*

*J*ERI WILLIAMS WAS BORN into the arms of a family without God. Driven to please, by age 30, as a business entrepreneur, she had reached every aspiration for financial gain, but her heart and home lay lifeless in the hollow emptiness of what the world calls success.

But God was faithful to answer the prayer of her great, great grandfather, that "the fires that burned within him would be her heritage." The zeal of this 1800's "Great Awakening" preacher of scriptural holiness looms in the fervent ministry of Jeri Williams as she heeds his call to "be careful in the rearing of your sons and daughters."

Today Jeri is called and anointed to awaken the hearts of families to hear what the Spirit has to say in these last days. Jeri compassionately expresses the yearning of the Holy Spirit to be welcomed in our homes, as she unfolds God's precious Word through teaching and worship arts.

Jeri is a wife, mother, songwriter, author, and minister. She has a B.A. degree in Psychology.